Substance and Essence
in Aristotle

Substance and Essence in Aristotle

An Interpretation of *Metaphysics* VII–IX

CHARLOTTE WITT

Cornell University Press

ITHACA AND LONDON

First published 1989 by Cornell University Press.
First printing, Cornell Paperbacks, 1994.

International Standard Book Number 0-8014-2126-8 (cloth)
International Standard Book Number 0-8014-8192-9 (paper)
Library of Congress Catalog Card Number 88-24043

Printed in the United States of America

*Librarians: Library of Congress cataloging information
appears on the last page of the book.*

♾ The paper in this book meets the minimum requirements of the
American National Standard for Information Sciences—Permanence
of Paper for Printed Library Materials, ANSI Z39.48-1984.

Paperback printing   10 9 8 7 6 5 4 3

To Mark

CONTENTS

ACKNOWLEDGMENTS

I began work on this book during a year spent on leave in Berkeley, California, and I thank the Philosophy and Classics departments at Berkeley for their hospitality. Special thanks go to Alan Code, Anthony Long, David Sedley, and Gregory Vlastos, who made my year more fruitful. I am very grateful to David Charles who read the entire manuscript twice; his comments and criticisms have helped produce a better book.

I owe a great deal to Mark Okrent, who saw this manuscript through any number of revisions. His criticisms, comments, and suggestions were invaluable, as was his unflagging support for my project. Most important, his involvement transformed the writing of this book from a lonely marathon into an extended philosophical discussion.

CHARLOTTE WITT

Portland, Maine

*Substance and Essence
in Aristotle*

INTRODUCTION

Essentialism, a controversial theory concerning the structure of reality, has both a rich past in the history of philosophy and new advocates—notably, Saul Kripke—among contemporary philosophers.[1] Essentialists believe that some constituents or properties of objects are essential to those objects, while other constituents or properties are not essential to them. There is an inner "core" or essence that constitutes the object and that cannot change so long as that object exists; the object might differ with respect to many of its features, but not with respect to its "core" or essence. Or so the story goes. In fact, I will argue that the differences between Aristotelian essentialism and Kripke's essentialism are so fundamental and pervasive that it is a serious distortion of both views to think of essentialism as a single theory that dons different garb in different historical periods.

Why is some version of the "story" I have sketched above

---

[1]For a sample of recent work on essentialism see Saul A. Kripke, *Naming and Necessity* (Cambridge: Harvard University Press, 1980); David Wiggins, *Sameness and Substance* (Cambridge: Harvard University Press, 1980); and *Midwest Studies in Philosophy XI: Studies in Essentialism*, ed. Peter French, Theodore E. Uehling, Jr., and Howard K. Wettstein (Minneapolis: University of Minnesota Press, 1986).

so widely believed by historians of philosophy and contemporary philosophers alike?[2] The reason is that, on a certain interpretation of Aristotle, the story is more or less true. I call this the "standard" interpretation, and I argue that on several basic issues the standard interpretation is mistaken. On the interpretation I propose in its place, important differences between Aristotelian essentialism and contemporary essentialism become visible. The body of this book is devoted to developing my interpretation of Aristotelian essentialism; in the last chapter, I explain some basic points of difference between Aristotle and Kripke. I believe that the contrast between Aristotle and Kripke helps us to understand each theory better and might even help us to think more clearly and precisely about essences.

What is the standard interpretation of Aristotelian essentialism, and how does my interpretation differ from it? The standard view runs along the following lines.[3] The most striking fact about individual substances such as Socrates and Bucephalus is that they are members of natural kinds or species (in this case, different species). Socrates is a human being, and Bucephalus is a horse. If you ask the question "What is Socrates?" the answer "a human being" leads directly to the Aristotelian notion of essence, for an Aristotelian essence is a nonlinguistic correlate of the definition of the entity in question. Specify what a human being is, and you will have specified Socrates' essence. On this interpretation, since Socrates and Plato are members of the same species, they share an essence that is also shared by all other human beings. This idea—i.e., a universal essence shared by all members of the

---

[2]The tendency on the part of contemporary essentialists to locate in Aristotle the historical origins of their essentialist views can be seen in Michael Slote, *Metaphysics and Essence* (Oxford: Blackwell, 1975), p. 1; Baruch Brody, *Identity and Essence* (Princeton: Princeton University Press, 1980), pp. 114–134; and Wiggins, *Sameness and Substance*. Interestingly, Kripke makes no historical connection between his essentialist views and Aristotle's.

[3]For differing versions of the standard interpretation, see Marjorie Grene, *A Portrait of Aristotle* (Chicago: University of Chicago Press, 1963), chap. 6; W. K. C. Guthrie, *A History of Greek Philosophy* (Cambridge: Cambridge University Press, 1981), vol. 6; and W. D. Ross, "Introduction," *Aristotle's Metaphysics* (Oxford: Clarendon Press, 1924), vol. 1.

same species—I call the *species-essence*. The standard interpretation holds that Aristotelian essences are species-essences. To explain the other striking fact about Socrates and Plato—namely, that they are individuals—the standard interpretation turns to the notion of matter. Matter is Aristotle's principle of individuation. The standard interpretation has the authority of tradition, makes sense, and enjoys textual support; nonetheless, I argue that it is mistaken on several basic points.

First, it is wrong in holding that the most important function of form or essence is to explain species membership. As I explain in Chapter 4, Aristotle describes form or essence as the cause of being of individual substances. What he means is that the form or essence is (i) the cause of there being an actual individual substance and (ii) the cause of its being a unity rather than a heap. That is to say, Aristotle's primary interest is in the question of what is responsible for the existence of an actual individual substance, rather than in the question of why we classify individual substances in the way that we do (i.e., into species).

Second, the traditional interpretation mistakenly holds that the essence of an individual, composite substance is universal rather then individual. In Chapter 5, I argue that for Aristotle the essences of individual substances (such as Socrates and Bucephalus) are individual rather than universal. The details of this argument will have to wait until later, but the basic point is that in the central books of the *Metaphysics* Aristotle maintains consistently that nothing universal can be substance, nor can it be a principle or cause of substance. But, if its form or essence is the cause of being of a substance, then clearly it is not universal, as the traditional account would have it.

Third, on my view, an essence is not a property (or a cluster of properties) of the substance whose essence it is. Socrates' essence is not a property of Socrates. My full argument for this claim is given in Chapter 4, but it turns on the idea that no property (no Aristotelian property) can be the cause of being of an actual, individual substance.

The second two points of difference between the traditional interpretation and my own have their origin in the first point of difference: namely, the different functions assigned to essence. For if the basic function of essence is to place individual substances into species, then what could serve this purpose better than an essence that is a universal property, shared by individuals of the same kind? If this were the role of essence in Aristotle's theory of substance, then the idea that essences are universal properties of substances would seem extremely plausible. But if, as I argue, this is not the function of Aristotelian essences, then the idea that essences are universal properties becomes less obvious. And if, in addition, there is substantial evidence against viewing essences as universal properties of substances, then there is good reason to reject the traditional interpretation.

The section of the *Metaphysics* with which we shall be primarily concerned, books vii–ix, has gained a deserved reputation as a difficult but engaging, apparently contradictory but profound, treatise. In the pages that follow, I do not discuss even these three books of the *Metaphysics* comprehensively. Rather, I focus on Aristotle's discussion of essence in relation to what he calls "sensible substances" (roughly speaking, the individual members of natural kinds).

Chapter 1 sets the stage, discussing the question of being in light of Aristotle's methodology and his conception of knowledge or understanding. In Chapter 2, I consider Aristotle's arguments for the priority of substances over the other categories of being in order to explain why he thinks one can study being by studying substance. Chapter 3 is devoted to a discussion of Aristotle's analysis of sensible substances, or individual members of natural kinds, into matter and form. This requires that we examine Aristotle's arguments in the *Physics* to the effect that an adequate explanation of the behavior of such substances must be given in terms of formal/final causation.

In Chapter 4, I draw together the lines of thought developed in the two preceding chapters with respect to the essences of sensible substances. I explain that the essence is the cause of being of the sensible substance, and I show that this means that essence is the cause of the existence and unity of the individual substance. Given this function, I argue, it is a mistake to think of the essence as a property of the substance. I also argue that, given Aristotle's view of the relationship between matter and form (or essence), it is also a mistake to think of the essence or form as a property of the matter. My interpretation of Aristotle's essences is completed in Chapter 5, where I argue that those essences are individuals and not universals. In Chapter 6, I introduce Kripke's theory of essences, contrasting his theory with my interpretation of Aristotle's essentialism.

This book is addressed primarily to readers with an interest in Aristotle's theory of essentialism, although it might also be of use to readers with an interest in contemporary essentialism. I did not write the book for specialists in Aristotle's thought, so it does not presume any knowledge of Greek or any familiarity with the *Metaphysics*. I wrote it to make a very difficult, but philosophically exciting, classic text accessible to the nonspecialist reader.

Although I have tried to write a book useful to a nonspecialist in Aristotelian metaphysics, I have not intended to level all the serious philosophical problems and issues of interpretation that abound in Aristotle's text. I have tried to develop the philosophical issues raised by Aristotle and, where appropriate, to indicate difficulties or shortcomings in his treatment of them. Further, some of the interpretations of Aristotle put forward in this book are controversial. On disputed points of interpretation I have tried to present a convincing argument for my view. Generally I leave any discussion of linguistic and textual matters, as well as alternative possible interpretations, for the notes.

Chapter 1

BEING

A glance at the table of contents of this book suggests that its central topic, Aristotle's essentialism, is not broached until the fourth chapter. Why are the earlier chapters devoted to other topics in Aristotle's metaphysics? There are two reasons. One is intelligibility: the material contained in this chapter, and in the following two, helps clarify what Aristotle says about essences—his ideas and the way he expresses those ideas. But there is another, more compelling, reason for beginning an account of Aristotle's essentialism by sketching out his approach to the question of being and his theory of substance, including his analysis of material substance. One of the theses of the last chapter in this book is that the precise form of Aristotle's essentialism, as opposed to other essentialist theories, results from the fact that the question of essences, for Aristotle, cannot be divorced from the investigation of being and substance. If this interpretation is correct (and I defer justification of the claim), then it would not be easy to understand the place and function of essences in Aristotle's thought without an understanding of his inquiry into being and substance. And the best approach to the investigation of substance is to begin with the question of being as it confronted Aristotle.

1. Aristotle's Approach to the Question of Being

Near the beginning of *Metaphysics* VII, Aristotle situates his inquiry into the nature of substance in relation to the traditional problem of being, and he implies that his investigation of substance will be influenced by the character of the historical enterprise:

> And indeed the question which was raised of old and now and always and which is always puzzled over, What is being?, is the question What is substance? For some say that it is one, some more than one, and some say that it is the limited and some the limitless. And so we, too, must investigate especially, and first, and exclusively, so to speak, concerning being described in this way, what it is.[1028b2-7][1]

This description of Aristotle's project has several interesting features that are important for the understanding of his discussions of substance in *Metaphysics* VII–IX.

One point of interest to us is the *kind* of answer offered by his predecessors to the being question. It is clear from the examples listed by Aristotle that they are not answering the question "What are the beings?" (or "What exists?"), for they do not offer an inventory of beings. They do not answer what I shall call "the population question," even though their answers clearly have some consequences for it. If, for example, like Parmenides, you hold that being is one, then at the same time you have a criterion for resolving the population question. Rather than answer the population question directly. Aristotle's predecessors provide a characterization of being; they answer the question "What is the nature of being?" Or, "What

---

[1]Except where noted, my translations are based on W. D. Ross's translation of the *Metaphysics*. In his commentary on this passage, Ross identifies those who say that being is one with the schools of Miletus (Thales) and Elea (Parmenides); those who say it is limited with the Pythagoreans and Empedocles; those who say it is limitless with Anaxagoras and the Atomists (*Aristotle's Metaphysics* [Oxford: Clarendon Press, 1924], vol. 2, p. 161).

is being like?" Aristotle follows their approach, and although
the population question with regard to substances is raised in
the chapter immediately following the quotation with which
I began (VII.1028b8–27; cf. VIII.1042a7–12), clearly Aristotle
thought that the final resolution of the population question
was posterior to an investigation of the nature of substance.
For, after he has recounted the extensive and diverse list of
entities that are thought to be substances (the candidates range
from the ordinary to the obscure), Aristotle says:

> Regarding these matters, then, we must inquire which of the
> common opinions are right and which are not right, and what
> things are substances, and whether there are or are not any
> besides sensible substances, and how sensible substances exist,
> and whether there is a separable substance (and if so why and
> how) or whether there is no substance separable from sensible
> substances; and we must first outline what substance is.
> [1028b27–32]

A final, complete answer to the population question depends
upon a prior answer to the definition question ("we must first
outline what substance is"). This ordering of the two questions
makes sense, since it is only when we know what substance
is that we can make a secure judgment concerning which things
are substances and which not. How can we proceed with
the definitional question? Aristotle proposes to investigate the
nature of substance by means of a study of a given population;
namely, sensible substances. Sensible substances such as individual horses or men are widely accepted as substances,
Aristotle says. Because they are noncontroversial exemplars,
they can be studied in order to understand what it is to be a
substance (VII.1029a33–34, VIII.1042a7–11).

I introduced the distinction between the population and definition questions as a means of disambiguating two ways of
taking the questions "What is being?" and "What is substance?" But, it is not at all clear what would count as an
adequate answer to the definitional question. Nor is it clear
how Aristotle thinks the definitional question ought to be answered. I have said that the final resolution of the population

question with regard to substances awaits an account of what substance is. And I have said that Aristotle embarks on an inquiry aimed at providing this account by examining sensible substances. As yet, however, I have not given any idea of the goal of the inquiry: namely, a specification of the kind of definition of substance Aristotle is seeking. I address this issue in § 5 of the present chapter.

A second interesting feature of this passage is that Aristotle connects the question "What is substance?" with a tradition of inquiry and perplexity over the nature of being. In Greek, each of the two words I have translated as "being" and "substance" is a form of the verb "to be." Thus, Aristotle's question "What is substance?" is a close linguistic relation to the tradition's "What is being?" Two features of Aristotle's depiction of the traditional response to this question are important for our understanding of his investigation of substance. On the one hand, Aristotle depicts earlier philosophers as diametrically opposed in their answers to the being question. On the other hand, Aristotle describes them as all puzzling over a single, basic question. There is a unity to their inquiries, a common question that he proposes to answer. In this passage, Aristotle is self-consciously taking as his subject matter the notion of being as defined by his predecessors, which means that his analysis begins with, and must do justice to, the views of earlier thinkers.[2]

[2]Aristotle's insistence on connecting his philosophical ideas with those of his predecessors is illustrated throughout the corpus. His historical description of the problem of being could be contrasted with numerous different approaches to philosophical topics. For the sake of brevity, I shall simply mention two alternative ways of thinking about philosophical problems and the philosophical tradition.

Rather than define a philosophical problem in terms of the views of earlier thinkers, some philosophers generate problems by constructing puzzling examples, or a series of such examples. These puzzling examples then constitute the subject matter of that area of philosophy. Although it might be possible to pluck these problems from historical sources, they are in principle ahistorical, and the entire problematic could be generated by a single philosopher. Philosophers who work this way obviously have a very different relation to their tradition than Aristotle had to his.

The phrase "being as defined by his predecessors" could cause confusion, especially in light of one current account of the origin of philosophical prob-

As we have seen, Aristotle takes an investigation of being as his subject matter in the central books of the *Metaphysics*. As an introduction to Aristotle's method of inquiry, it is helpful to note two important features of his description of how that investigation of being is connected with earlier efforts. First, it is a subject that has been puzzled over, is being puzzled over, and will continue to be puzzled over. Second, it is a subject matter that Aristotle approaches through a consideration of the opinions of earlier philosophers. These two points are related because the puzzling over being in the past has generated the opinions that Aristotle takes as a starting point for his inquiry. These two features of Aristotle's approach to the question of being are very important because they define his project by explaining his starting point and his methodology.

What exactly *is* Aristotle's starting point and methodology, his approach to being? Aristotle begins his investigation of being with the opinions of his predecessors. But, as pointed out, those opinions differ widely; indeed, they contradict one another. If you begin with such opinions (e.g., being is one, being is many), how do you proceed? The first step, Aristotle tells us in book III of the *Metaphysics*, is to state and develop the topics that need puzzling over with regard to being. Some of the issues—e.g., is being one or many?—arise directly from a survey of the opinions of earlier thinkers on the nature of being; others, perhaps, did not occur to Aristotle's predecessors, and those Aristotle himself must develop (995a24–27).

What Aristotle actually does in book III is to state and develop arguments in favor of each of the opposing ways of thinking

---

lems. One might think that Aristotle begins with the views of his predecessors just because the notion of being is a concept that exists within the tradition. On this view, being is a concept or idea that exists in a series of philosophical texts. To investigate being is just to investigate an idea within a world and tradition of philosophical writings. Although this is a possible view of the philosophical tradition and its role in generating and sustaining philosophical problems and topics, it is not Aristotle's view. Aristotle begins with the views of earlier philosophers not because his topic is the concept of "being" in the tradition, but because he wants to incorporate their understanding of being into his own inquiry. And he wants to do so because he thinks that prior thinkers have made progress toward an understanding of being.

about the principles of being. The puzzlement arises precisely because there *are* considerations on both sides of a given issue. If one is presented with arguments on both sides of an issue, the first reaction is to feel mentally blocked. Aristotle's metaphor for this state of intellectual impasse is the body being tied up or bound, (995a31–33) and he describes subsequent forward movement or facility of thought as following upon the untying of the mental knot. The term for this sort of mental puzzle is *aporia*, which has the connotation of "a blocked path or passage."

The intellect is bound by the considerations for and against a given position. However, Aristotle thinks that this stage is unavoidable; indeed, it is a necessary preliminary for an adequate resolution of the intellectual dilemma. If one wants to resolve puzzles, Aristotle says, it is necessary to understand the puzzles. What is it to understand a puzzle? It is to grasp fully the considerations on both sides of an issue. If one has done this, one understands the depth of the difficulty. One cannot figure out a solution to a problem one does not fully understand. In the first place, it is only through a statement of the difficulties that one can envision what an adequate solution would have to look like. In addition, hearing the arguments or evidence in favor of different positions places one in a better position to make a decision (995a33–995b4).

In the *Topics*, Aristotle calls the reasoning from generally accepted opinions or beliefs "dialectical reasoning" (100a30). He explains that the generally accepted beliefs are "those which commend themselves to all or to the majority or to the wise— that is, to all of the wise or to the majority or to the most famous or distinguished of them" (100b21–23). Dialectical reasoning proceeds from these starting points, and the *Topics* outlines strategies for developing arguments from them. In the *Topics*, Aristotle lists two ways in which dialectic is useful for the philosophical sciences. First, dialectic is helpful in determining truth and falsehood, for "if we are able to raise difficulties on both sides, we shall more easily discern truth and falsehood on every point" (101a34–36). Second, dialectic enables one to reason about the first principles of the various

sciences, including, presumably, the science of being. I discuss
the relationship between the science of being and first principles more fully in §§ 3 and 4 below. For the present discussion,
it is sufficient to say that Aristotle assigns to the science of
being the role of investigating first principles.

In light of the similarity between this description of dialectic
and Aristotle's approach to being in the *Metaphysics*, is it correct
to call Aristotle's science of being "dialectic"? It is not—for the
simple reason that in the *Metaphysics* Aristotle differentiates
philosophy from dialectic in terms of the kind of capacity involved, i.e., what each can achieve. For in relation to the same
domain, i.e., being, dialectic is only tentative or critical,
whereas philosophy is able to know (1004b22–26). This mark
of difference concerns what is achieved by dialectic and philosophy. It does not concern the narrower question of methodology—i.e., the procedure of beginning with the opinions
of the wise or the many, then elaborating the pros and cons
attaching to those positions. Rather, philosophy and dialectic
differ on another point: philosophy, or the science of being,
achieves truth and knowledge; dialectic does not. The fact that
Aristotle differentiates philosophy and dialectic on this point
alone supports the interpretation that they share a methodology in the narrower sense.

A natural question follows. Given that philosophy and dialectic share a methodology in the narrow sense, why do they
differ in result? According to the Cartesian account of philosophical methodology, the situation just described is impossible, for a method is simply a set of rules that ensure positive,
consistent results if followed diligently. Hence, it would be
impossible for the same approach or method to be employed
and not achieve the same results. On this view, if dialectic and
the science of being differ in that one achieves knowledge and
the other does not, then they cannot be following the same
procedures. For Aristotle, however, it is the structure of what
is known that makes a group of propositions knowledge or
science, not whether they are the result of following a certain
method of inquiry. It is not the kind of reasoning or the method
that makes a body of propositions a science but, rather, that

the propositions be of a certain kind and have certain relationships to one another. So, the philosopher can reason dialectically and yet differ from the dialectician, in that the
philosopher achieves knowledge and the dialectician does not.
Science can be the result of reasoning dialectically, even if that
is not what makes it science. In Aristotle's framework, then,
the difference between the science of being and dialectic can
be specified quite independently from the obvious points of
similarity.[3]

I have said that, for Aristotle, what makes a body of propositions a science is not that it is the fruit of a favored method
or procedure (e.g., Aristotelian dialectic or the Cartesian
method of doubt). Rather, a body of propositions is or is not
a science just because it has a certain structure. In the *Posterior
Analytics*, Aristotle spells out the scientific structure in some
detail: Aristotelian science is demonstrative; it proceeds from
necessary, immediate first principles, and so on. It would take
us very far off the track, however, to consider the important
features of Aristotelian science in any detail.[4] What is germane
to the issue at hand—namely, how dialectic and philosophy
differ—can be seen without even a summary of the contents
of the *Posterior Analytics*. All one needs to know is that Aristotle's specification of what a science is, and hence of what
knowledge is, does not consist of a description of a particular
method of inquiry, nor is a particular method of inquiry part
of Aristotle's specification of what a science is.[5]

---

[3]*Aristotle on Dialectic*, ed. G. E. L. Owen (Oxford: Clarendon Press, 1968)
contains a number of useful papers on dialectic in the *Topics*. For a full discussion of dialectic in Aristotle, see J. D. G. Evans, *Aristotle's Concept of Dialectic*
(Cambridge: Cambridge University Press, 1977). I disagree with Evans's account of the basis for the sharp distinction between dialectic and what he calls
"the universal science of ontology" (p. 5).

[4]Myles Burnyeat's "Aristotle on Understanding Knowledge," in *Aristotle on
Science: The Posterior Analytics*, ed. E. Berti (Padua: Editrice Antenore, 1981),
contains a clear and compelling account of Aristotelian science.

[5]In "Aristotle's Discovery of Metaphysics" (*Review of Metaphysics*, 31 [Dec.
1977], 210–229) Terence Irwin discusses the problems surrounding the question
of whether or not dialectic is the method for the science of being. He is particularly good in explaining the tensions between dialectic and the description
of science in the *Analytics*. It is important to mention one point from his paper.

Although I do not intend to embark on a general discussion of Aristotelian epistemology at this point, it will be useful to give further consideration to Aristotle's notions of science and knowledge, especially as these are relevant to his investigation of being. For it is difficult to envision the goal of Aristotle's inquiry into being, which is a science of being, without an understanding of the basic concepts of Aristotelian epistemology.

2. What Is It to Know Something?

An initial question about Aristotle's epistemology concerns terminology. For, in the preceding section, I have used the terms "science" and "knowledge" alternately, as if they were interchangeable, and together, as if they were equivalent. This does not follow our current philosophical practice, which distinguishes between knowledge and science, and which classifies science as one kind or species of knowledge. With the words "science" and "knowledge" I am translating a single Aristotelian term: *epistēmē*. Although in some contexts it is more perspicuous to translate *epistēmē* as "knowledge," and in others as "science," it is common practice to translate the term by the phrase "scientific knowledge." The reason is that Aristotle's characterization of *epistēmē* does not coincide with current characterizations of knowledge, so it would be quite confusing to translate *epistēmē* simply as "knowledge."[6] Indeed, it is the difference between our notion of knowledge and Aristotle's *epistēmē* that translators attempt to capture with the term "science" or the modifier "scientific." But which distinctive features of Aristotelian *epistēmē* (which I will continue to translate

---

Irwin argues that while dialectic might get to first principles, it could never establish them as first principles, i.e., as true and necessary (pp. 214–215). My account of the difference between dialectic and science ignores this point in detaching the method from the results of the method. Irwin would argue that this leaves a lacuna: namely, an account of the special epistemological status of the first principles.

[6]The word "ἐπιστήμη" in Aristotle is best translated as "knowledge" or "science," depending upon the context. That the translation "science" is appropriate here should become clear as this chapter progresses.

either as "knowledge" or as "science," or both, depending upon context) are important for our understanding of Aristotle's conception of a science of being?

Three crucial features of Aristotle's conception of knowledge are directly relevant to his investigation of being and substance: (i) the idea that knowledge is of principles and causes; (ii) the idea that wisdom, or the highest form of knowledge, requires a grasp of *first* principles and causes; and (iii) the idea that knowledge is systematic. The first feature amounts to the position that knowledge is explanatory. For Aristotle, to know something is to understand it, and to understand something is to grasp its principles or causes. The second point is that knowledge, since it is explanatory, necessitates a grasp of *first* principles and causes, because knowledge of what is explained by a principle requires an understanding of that principle. And that principle, in turn, is understood through another principle—and so on, until the first principles are reached. The third feature is a consequence of the first two. Knowledge, for Aristotle, does not come in discrete bits; rather, it consists of the grasp of a connected body of truths. Knowledge is explanatory, and, as we have seen, our grasp of any part of the system depends ultimately upon our grasp of the first principles. The phrase "body of knowledge" describes the systematic nature of Aristotelian *epistēmē*.

One place where these three features of Aristotle's concept of knowledge are presented is in *Metaphysics* i, where Aristotle discusses both the nature of knowledge in general and the nature of the highest form of knowledge, which he there calls "wisdom" or "philosophy." This discussion is of particular use to us, since it occurs in the context of Aristotle's informal introduction to the investigation of being. One of his purposes in the first two chapters is to explain the three characteristics of knowledge outlined above. Let us consider them in more detail.

The first feature of Aristotelian knowledge or science is that it is constituted by a grasp of principles and causes. To know something, Aristotle claims, is to know *why* it is or happened, not merely that it is or happened. I will consider Aristotle's justification for this position in a moment. First, though, we need to know what Aristotle means by the terms *archē* (translated "principle") and *aitia* (translated "cause"). In particular, we need to know how Aristotelian *archai* and *aitiai* differ from principles and causes, as we now conceive of them. For, notwithstanding the standard translations, an Aristotelian *archē* is not exactly a principle, as we think of one, and an Aristotelian *aitia* is even less like our modern, post-Humean notion of a cause. These differences are immediately apparent in Aristotle's discussions of the uses of the two terms in *Metaphysics* v, a book often referred to as Aristotle's philosophical lexicon (see chapters 1 and 2).

A principle, as we think of it today, is a rule, a law, or a basic truth.[7] An Aristotelian *archē*, in contrast, means an "origin" or "source", and bears traces of its nonphilosophical usage in which it means a "ruler" (1012b34–1013a16). The notion of an *archē* as an origin or source, in particular, flavors Aristotle's summary of the uses of the term: "It is common, then, to all principles to be the first point from which a thing either is or comes to be or is known; but some of these are immanent in the thing and others are outside" (1013a17–20).

What intuitive difference is there between the idea of a rule, or law, and the idea of an origin or source? Rules and laws are regulative notions: the behavior of entities is governed (or ought to be governed) by them. An origin or source, in contrast, is more loosely tied to the notion of regulation (where an entity comes from might or might not govern its behavior). The idea of an origin or source carries with it another association, the idea of dependence, which is not associated with the notion of a rule or law. A child comes from, and is dependent upon, its parents. Aristotle's statement, in the last quotation, that some principles are internal to the entity and some are external to it, makes sense if we understand "principle" to mean "source" or "origin," but it does not make sense if we under-

---

[7]In fact, a very good etymological dictionary will cite "source or origin" as a meaning of "principle," but today this meaning is neither in general use nor in philosophical use.

stand it to mean "rule" or "law." A child's parents are its external source of generation, its *archai*, but it sounds peculiar to characterize them as rules or laws. In order for many of Aristotle's comments about principles to make sense, it is crucial to think of an Aristotelian principle as an origin or source of something, not as a rule or law or basic truth.

The differences between an Aristotelian *aitia* and the modern notion of a cause have been written about extensively.[8] Indeed, to anyone influenced by the post-Humean notion of a cause, Aristotle's description of his four causes will scarcely seem to be a description of *causes* at all:

> We call a cause (1) that from which (as immanent material) a thing comes into being, e.g., the bronze of the statue and the silver of the saucer, and the classes which include these. (2) The form or pattern, i.e., the formula of the essence, and the classes which include this (e.g., the ratio 2:1 and number in general are causes of the octave) and the parts of the formula. (3) That from which the change or the freedom from change first begins; e.g., the man who has deliberated is a cause, and the father is a cause of the child, and in general the maker a cause of the thing made and the change-producing of the changing. (4) The end, i.e., that for the sake of which a thing is; e.g., health is the cause of walking. For why does one walk? We say "in order that one may be healthy," and in speaking thus we think we have given the cause. [1013a24–35]

In order of their presentation, then, Aristotle's four causes are the material cause, the formal cause, the efficient cause, and the final cause. Two basic features of Aristotle's four causes are difficult to reconcile with our modern notion of a cause. First, the entities mentioned as causes are objects rather than events (the standard causal items in post-Humean accounts of causality). Second, some of the objects mentioned (e.g., those posited as formal and final causes) do not seem to be the kinds of entities that could be causes at all. According to Hume's

---

[8]See, for example, Richard Sorabji, *Necessity, Cause, and Blame* (Ithaca: Cornell University Press, 1980); and Michael Frede, "The Original Notion of Cause," in *Essays in Ancient Philosophy* (Minneapolis: University of Minnesota Press, 1987), pp. 125–150.

analysis, for one thing, a cause is supposed to precede its effect; it is hard to see how an Aristotelian final cause, a goal or end, could meet this requirement.

I discuss Aristotle's four causes in more detail in Chapter 3. For present purposes, i.e., to understand Aristotle's view that knowledge is of principles and causes, it is sufficient to keep in mind the ways in which an Aristotelian *aitia* differs from the modern notion of a cause. On the positive side, it is helpful to think of the four causes as those factors responsible for the generation of an entity.[9] In the generation of a human being, for example, the formal cause is the human form carried by the sperm from the male; the material cause is the menstrual fluid contributed by the female; the efficient cause is the motions in the sperm from the male (or, Aristotle says, one could also call the male the efficient cause); and the final cause is the end of the generation (in this case, the production of a human offspring).[10] These four factors, together, are responsible for the generation of a human being.

A final point, concerning the relationship between Aristotelian principles and causes, illustrates and supports the idea that these terms have to be understood differently from the way that we usually understand them today. For it is clear that principles and causes are very closely connected in Aristotle's thought, and yet there is no close connection between a principle, thought of as a rule, and the modern conception of a cause, which is an event. Aristotle's common practice is to use the terms "principle" and "cause" interchangeably (the first book of the *Metaphysics* is crowded with such instances). Further, Aristotle's explicit comments on the relationship between principle and cause describe a very close connection. In one place, he says that all

---

[9] In fact, the theory is introduced in the *Physics* as an account of the factors involved in the generation and destruction of a *natural* being. I explain what a natural being is, for Aristotle, and discuss his four causes further in Chapter 3.

[10] One of the alternative efficient causes in this list ("the motions in the semen") appears to consist of events rather than to be an object. But, as I said earlier in this chapter, Aristotle standardly lists objects (e.g., the male parent) as efficient causes. For a discussion of this nonstandard description of an efficient cause see Chapter 3, note 13.

causes are principles (1013a16–17); in another, he says that principle and cause follow from one another (i.e., logically imply one another). But he insists that they do not share a definition (1003b22–25). Anything that is a principle is a cause and vice versa, but what it is to be a principle differs from what it is to be a cause. There is no similar close connection between principles and causes in our current philosophical idiom. Not only do "principle" and "cause" differ in definition, but neither do they logically imply one another. If we keep in mind what I have said about Aristotelian principles and causes, and think about Aristotle's explanation of the generation of a child in terms of the four causes, it is perfectly obvious why he would also call them "principles." A principle is an origin or source of something (in this case, a generation), and the four causes are the principles, the sources of the offspring.

We are now sufficiently familiar with Aristotle's terminology to pose a question concerning his claim that we should understand all knowledge as requiring a grasp of causes and principles. Let us accept Aristotle's analysis of generation in terms of the four causes. Why does Aristotle think that all knowledge, including the highest cognitive state, wisdom, is constituted by a grasp of causes and principles? Does it not make perfectly good sense, for example, to say that I know there was a generation, because I observed it, even though I do not at all grasp its causes?

In *Metaphysics* I, chapters 1 and 2, Aristotle justifies his position by an appeal to ordinary judgment, arguing that most people identify wisdom and every other body of knowledge with the knowledge of causes and principles, not with the knowledge of facts. This distinction needs clarification. For Aristotle, both the knowledge of principles and causes and what I have called "knowledge of facts" are factual in the sense that they correspond with the way the world is. Causes and principles, it should be remembered throughout this discussion, are real; they are not explanatory devices for Aristotle (I elaborate on this point in Chapter 3). Still, the question remains: Why is knowledge identified with causes and principles and not with facts?

Aristotle adduces various sorts of evidence to the effect that people believe that a person who knows causes has knowledge. The core of Aristotle's argument, however, is his distinction between persons of experience and persons of knowledge. His ranking of cognizers runs from persons who operate simply on the basis of sense perception, through persons who have experience, to those who have knowledge (981b29–982a3). Knowledge is further divided into two classes: theoretical knowledge and productive or practical knowledge. The critical distinction for our purposes is that between persons of experience and persons of knowledge or art, for such a distinction is between persons who do not know the cause and persons who do know. For simplicity's sake, I shall contrast the knower and the experienced person, and ignore the distinction between practical and theoretical knowers. The important point is this: both kinds of knowers are knowers through the grasp of causes and principles, and in this respect they differ from persons of experience. Once Aristotle has established this point, he proceeds to identify wisdom with the knowledge of specific principles and causes: namely, the first or highest principles and causes (981b27–29).

What, then, *is* the difference between a person of experience and a person of art or knowledge, according to Aristotle? What picture of knowledge emerges from this distinction? Aristotle lists two basic features to account for the difference: (i) the knower, unlike the person of experience, can make a universal judgment rather than a singular judgment or series of singular judgments; (ii) the knower grasps the cause, *the why*, but the person of experience grasps only the fact, or *the that*. To illustrate this distinction, Aristotle refers to the art of medicine.[11]

_____

[11]Aristotle illustrates his point from medicine by using a classification of human constitutions that was probably familiar to his audience. G. E. R. Lloyd, in *Magic, Reason, and Experience: Studies in the Origin and Development of Greek Science* (Cambridge: Cambridge University Press, 1979), presents evidence from the Hippocratic corpus of a tendency to attribute a causal role to the constitution of the body in connection with disease (see p. 146ff.). Lloyd also records that the treatise *On the Nature of Man* argues for a four-humor theory, which included the phlegmatic and bilious constitutions (p. 149). In addition, Lloyd notes that the treatise *On the Sacred Disease* claims that the

He contrasts two sorts of judgment made by two kinds of doctors. One doctor operates on the basis of experience (E), whereas the other has grasped the cause (K):

> (E) When Callias had a fever, remedy *y* was effective.
> When Socrates had a fever, remedy *y* was effective, etc.
>
> (K) When any person with a phlegmatic character has a fever, remedy *y* is effective.

One difference between these two sorts of judgment has received much comment: namely, that the knower makes a universal judgment, but the person of experience is limited to listing his or her experience. How is Aristotle's other basis for his distinction reflected in these examples? Why is it only the knower who grasps the cause? After all, both persons could give reasons for acting a certain way when faced with a feverish person. The person of experience has a reason for giving remedy *y*: it has worked in the past in a similar situation. The crucial difference is that the knower understands *why* the remedy works and, therefore, can give a reason in a stronger sense for his action, i.e., a reason stronger than the fact that remedy *y* has worked in the past. In this case, the reason the remedy works is that the person has a certain constitution, so the person of art has grasped a systematic relationship among a given constitution, a given illness, and a given remedy. When one understands why the remedy has worked in the cases in which it did, one's knowledge is universal; for one also knows quite generally when it will work.[12] The fact that the doctor who has

---

disease in question (epilepsy) occurs in the phlegmatic, but not the bilious (p. 20). The distinction between these two sorts of constitutions is basic to an argument in the treatise concerning the cause of epilepsy; the author argues that the disease could not be divinely caused, for it affects people differently according to their constitutions.

[12] We find a similar contrast between experience and the knowledge of principles in other ancient philosophical texts. According to Sextus Empiricus, empirical doctors carry on their medical practice without knowledge of first principles (*Adv. Math.* VIII. 191, 327). From Plato we get the information that, much to the scorn of the empirical doctor, the logical physician is prone to talk to the patient in order to ascertain the origin of the disease and the constitution of the body (*Laws* 857c). Finally, in the *Gorgias*, Plato contrasts

knowledge forms a universal judgment is a consequence of the fact that he or she knows the cause.

The person of experience grasps only *the that*, the fact. However vast one's experience, one's only justification for a given judgment appeals to just that prior experience itself. One is restricted to the facts, even if one can draw on a large body of recorded experience on a given matter. The facts in question need not be, and most often are not, restricted to direct experience. For us, this seems like a perfectly adequate form of justification (namely, induction), and we are perfectly happy to say that such a person knows, if the evidence is correctly related to the conclusion. Aristotle, however, is clearly reserving the terms "knowledge" (or "science") and "art" for another epistemic state. The knower can make a universal statement not because of an extensive body of experience or evidence, but because he or she has understood the cause of the phenomena in question.[13] Knowing the cause, or *the why*, makes universal judgments possible and not the other way around.[14]

---

those endeavors which are arts with those which are pursued through experience and habit (463b, 465a). Socrates explains why cookery is an experience and not an art as follows: "And I say it is not an art but an experience because it has no account to give of the real nature of the things to which it applies and so cannot tell the cause of any of them" (465b). In order to grasp the cause, one must understand the real nature of the thing in question. In the example we have been analyzing from Aristotle, one must grasp the underlying constitution of the patient.

[13]Experience *does* have an important role to play in the genesis of an Aristotelian science. Experience supplies the principles peculiar to each science. For example, astronomical experience provides the principles, the starting points, of astronomical science: "It falls to experience to provide the principles of any subject. In astronomy, for instance, it was astronomical experience that provided the principles of the science, for it was only when the phenomena were adequately grasped that the proofs in astronomy were discovered. And the same is true of any art or science whatever" (*An. Pr.* 46a17–22).

The massing of observation is a necessary condition for the development of a science such as astronomy. But astronomical knowledge or science is a systematic account of the causes of the phenomena. That is to say, astronomical science consists of a body of propositions appropriately related to one another. Dialectic plays the role for philosophy that experience plays in relation to astronomical science.

[14]My emphasis on the importance of the cause is compatible with, and helps to explain, Aristotle's other remarks about the differences between experience and knowledge or art in *Metaphysics* I. 1–2. When Aristotle says that experience

Aristotle is confident that, once he has explained the difference between grasping facts and grasping causes, his audience will agree that knowledge is constituted by the grasping of causes. The fact that Aristotle writes as if he is simply developing the connotations of the term *epistēmē* in a systematic manner is illuminating, for it suggests that the term has connotations our current philosophical notion of knowledge does not share. A person who has *epistēmē* grasps the cause of a given phenomenon, can make a universal judgment about it, can explain it, and can teach others about it.

The second crucial feature of Aristotle's conception of knowledge is his notion that the highest form of knowledge, wisdom or philosophy, is the grasp of *first* principles and causes. Every science or art—practical, productive, or theoretical—consists of an understanding of principles and causes. The doctor who knows does so because he or she understands the causes of disease, the architect who knows understands the principles of building, and the mathematician similarly knows his or her domain. The highest form of knowledge, which Aristotle calls in chapters 1 and 2 of the *Metaphysics* "wisdom" or "philosophy," is distinguished from other arts and sciences by being the grasp of the first, or highest, principles and causes.

In a passage heavy with Platonic overtones, Aristotle explains and justifies this claim by appealing to the characteristics of a wise person, a philosopher (982a6–19). A wise person knows all things through a knowledge of universals, is not restricted to objects of sense but knows difficult things, and can teach their causes to others. Further, the wise person understands theoretical, as opposed to practical, subjects and un-

---

is not inferior to art with respect to action, and is actually better than theory without experience, he explains by pointing out that experience is knowledge of individuals, that art is knowledge of universals, and that the actions are always directed toward individuals (981a12–24). The doctor in our example cures individuals with a specific constitution, not the constitution itself. If the doctor knows the causal relationship among illness, constitution, and cure, but cannot identify an instance of the constitution in question, then he or she will be unable to apply that knowledge and will be less useful than an empirical doctor who lacks knowledge of the cause of the disease but can prescribe a treatment based on experience.

derstands the highest and most authoritative sciences. Since the wise person pursues knowledge for its own sake, and not for its practical rewards, he or she is interested in what can be truly known, in the most knowable objects. And the most knowable things are the first principles and causes (982a29–b2). They are the most knowable, Aristotle says, because "by reason of these, and from these, all other things are known, but these are not known by means of the things subordinate to them" (982b2–4). Grasp of the first principles will provide an understanding of everything explained by them, and so the wise person will have a universal understanding.

The Aristotelian picture of philosophy as concerned with understanding first principles makes sense on the assumption that knowledge is systematic. This is the third characteristic of knowledge that we noted above as being particularly pertinent to Aristotle's investigation of being. To say that knowledge is systematic, in this context, means three things. First, bodies of knowledge, or sciences, are internally structured according to the picture painted in the *Posterior Analytics*. For our purposes, the central feature of such a portrait of science is that knowledge is of principles and causes. Second, philosophy or wisdom is also thought of as consisting of a grasp of causes, but in this case the causes in question are first causes. Third, knowledge or science does not consist of a series of entirely independent disciplines, or bodies of knowledge; for it is the philosopher who grasps the first principles who is described by Aristotle as thereby knowing all things.

When Aristotle speaks of having "knowledge" of a systematic body of principles or causes, he is using that term in a general sense and does not address the issues peculiar to *philosophical* knowledge. Philosophy, or wisdom, enters into the picture as the highest form of knowledge, consisting of a grasp of the highest or first principles and causes. But this simple picture neglects important issues for the understanding of philosophical knowledge. Is philosophical knowledge (the science of being) different from other kinds of knowledge or science in any important respects? Exactly how is the science of being related to other bodies of knowledge? We shall explore these questions in the next two sections.

3. The Science of Being

I will now discuss Aristotle's description of philosophical knowledge in two important texts of the *Metaphysics*. In these texts, Aristotle refers to philosophical knowledge (what he calls "wisdom" or "philosophy" in the texts discussed in the last section) as the "science of being *qua* being" or "first philosophy." We shall focus on two issues: (i) how the science of being differs from other sciences or bodies of knowledge and (ii) how it is related to them.

In the opening lines of *Metaphysics* VI, Aristotle says:

> We are seeking the principles and the causes of beings, and obviously of them insofar as they are. For, while there is a cause of health and of good condition, and the objects of mathematics have first principles and elements and causes, and in general every science which is ratiocinative or at all involves reasoning deals with causes and principles, more or less precise, all these sciences mark off some particular being—some genus—and inquire into this, but not into being simply nor insofar as it is, nor do they offer any discussion of the "what is it" of the things of which they treat; but starting from the "what is it" making it plain to the senses—others assuming it as a hypothesis—they then demonstrate, more or less cogently, the *per se* attributes of the genus with which they deal. [1025b3–13]

Every science investigates causes and principles. A particular science is directed toward a particular genus of being, and it begins with two assumptions: namely, the existence of the genus and the definition (the "what is it") of the genus it studies. For example, the science of arithmetic posits the existence and definition of units, and geometry posits the existence and definition of points and lines (*An. Post.* 1.10.76b3–6). As becomes clear in the rest of VI.1, Aristotle begins by mentioning these features of ordinary science in order to contrast them with the science of being; for when Aristotle turns to the science of being, neither of these assumptions is made. The science of being does not begin with a definite genus to study. Indeed, whether there are immovable substances, whether first philosophy is equivalent to physics (the study of nature) or not, whether the highest theoretical science is truly universal (or instead studies one genus), and the question of the essence or definition of being are all left open at the outset (1026a23–32). These questions are at the heart of the investigation of being. The science of being differs from other sciences in that it does not take for granted either the genus it studies (the answer to the population question) or the essence of what it studies (the answer to the definitional question).

But what does the science of being study? After all, each science studies beings (e.g., mathematics studies mathematical beings). Imagine that all human knowledge has been codified into ten sciences or bodies of knowledge that exhaust the possible objects of knowledge. Why is it that the science of being is not simply the sum total of the individual sciences of the various sorts of beings? Such an approach would be inadequate because what is sought are the principles of being itself, not the sum of the principles of the different genera of beings. For the principles that beings have as mathematical cannot be totaled up with other kinds of principles in order to arrive at the principles of being. The principles that attach to beings in the different sciences do not belong to the objects as beings but, rather, as quantities and so forth. A sum of such principles, even if all sciences were considered, would not amount to a set of principles of being; for none of the original principles was a principle of being but, rather, was a principle of a genus of being (e.g., the mathematical). Aristotle expresses this point by saying that the science of being investigates the principles and causes of beings *qua* being, or beings insofar as they are beings.

Aristotle's statements and arguments to the effect that being is not a genus can be viewed as exemplifying the point I have just made concerning the science of being.[15] For

---

[15]In his *aporia* concerning whether the highest or lowest genera should be

with respect to the problem of subject matter, one might want to say that there is an easy solution: namely, to conceive of being itself as a genus, the most universal genus. As we shall see in the next chapter, Aristotle does not take this alternative because he does not think that being has one meaning for all categories; there is no universal science of being because, for entities in different categories, what it is to be differs. However, the consideration of whether or not one should conceive of being as a genus and as the subject matter of first philosophy—exactly as mathematical objects are the genus and subject matter of the mathematical science—is an appropriate question for first philosophy. And there is no parallel question for mathematics. (See the explicit contrast between mathematics and the philosophical science on this point at 1005a11–18.)

Aristotle's description of the science of being in book iv, chapter 1, of the *Metaphysics* adds another distinctive characteristic to this science in contrast to other sciences. Not only do other sciences make the assumptions just mentioned concerning their subject matters, but they also take for granted the formal notions that determine what a science is. They do not inquire into such notions as "priority" or "genus", for example. The science of being, says Aristotle, does both (1005a13). The *aporiai* (or puzzles) concerning the nature of the principles of being, which I discuss in the next section, exemplify the way in which the investigation into being includes an investigation into the formal notions used in achieving an understanding of being. In other words, part of the science of being, part of what

---

identified as the principles of beings, Aristotle makes the following argument to the effect that being is not a genus: "But it is not possible that either unity or being should be the genus of beings; for the differentiae of any genus must each of them both have being or be one, but it is not possible for the genus to be predicated of the differentiae taken apart from the species (any more than for the species of the genus to be predicated of its proper differentiae;) so that if unity or being is a genus, no differentia will have being or be one" (998b22–27). If being were a genus, Aristotle argues, then it could not be predicated of the various differentiae of the genus, and hence the differentiae would not be beings. In the *Topics*, Aristotle argues that the genus cannot be predicated of the differentiae because, if it were, then the differentiae would themselves be individuals or species (144a36–b3).

is in question, concerns what it is to be a science, for Aristotle assigns to first philosophy the task of raising questions about those notions which are used to frame the Aristotelian concept of science.

The science of being differs from other bodies of knowledge or sciences in two ways. Unlike other sciences, first philosophy reflects on its subject matter and it investigates the structure of science by investigating those concepts which determine the notion of a science. The difference between the science of being and other sciences is not simply that the science of being has a different subject matter from other sciences, as it obviously does, nor is it that it has a different conception of science. Rather, it is that, unlike the aim of other sciences, the task of first philosophy is to reason about its subject matter and its principles, and about the nature of subject matters and first principles in general (i.e., the structure of knowledge and science). It is the self-reflective character of the science of being, as exemplified in its attitude toward its subject matter and its character as a science, that is the deepest point of difference between it and other sciences.

How is first philosophy, or the science of being, related to other forms of inquiry and bodies of knowledge? In the last section, the picture was of a science of first principles that would be a universal science because first principles are those shared by all entities. This very sketchy picture of the position of first philosophy in relation to other sciences raises important questions concerning their exact relationship. Does Aristotle hold, as some have interpreted Plato as holding, that philosophy proves or establishes the principles of other disciplines for them?[16] If not, what important role does first philosophy

---

[16]This mention of Plato is necessarily brief and dogmatic, although the interpretations suggested are not idiosyncratic. In a celebrated passage at the end of *Republic* vi, Plato sketches out a hierarchy of knowledge that shares the second characteristic attributed to Aristotle's concept of knowledge: knowledge is systematic and holistic; the Forms are grasped not atomistically, but in their relations to one another. Dialectic is systematic in that it considers Forms in relation to one another (*Rep.* 511c). Further, Forms are to be understood in relation to the Good (505a, 532ab). For Plato, knowledge is also knowledge of causes. Right opinion is differentiated from knowledge in that the latter in-

play in relation to other sciences? In what sense is it true to say that the science of first principles is a universal science?

In the texts we have been considering, there is little support for the view that the first philosopher is given the task of proving or establishing the first principles of the other disciplines. For example, Aristotle does not assign to first philosophy the twin task of establishing the existence of the genus of mathematical science and demonstrating its definitions.[17] So, we ought to reject the picture of the first philosopher as a polymath, busily providing the principles for every systematic body of knowledge. We must attach another sense to the idea that the person who knows the first principles knows universally.

The description of the science of being in the texts under consideration suggests another picture of the relationship between the highest science and the other sciences. There are certain basic concepts, common to all sciences, that it falls to the philosopher to investigate. The reflections of first philosophy on such important formal notions as the "same" and the "similar" and their opposites, as well as on notions such as

---

cludes "an account of the cause" (*Meno* 97d). In the *Republic*, Plato considers inferior those disciplines (e.g., mathematics) that are based on hypothetical starting points; they do not establish or render unhypothetical their own starting points (510b, 511b). Another way of stating Plato's point is that they never transform their hypotheses into genuine first principles, principles that are no longer hypothetical. Dialectic, by contrast, begins with what is hypothetical, but ascends to an unhypothetical first principle (511b). Under one interpretation of these passages from the *Republic*, Plato is held to have envisioned philosophy as providing the ground for the hypothetical starting points of such sciences as mathematics. Under this interpretation, Plato holds not just that knowledge is systematic, but that all branches of knowledge are unified and rooted in philosophical knowledge. Philosophy grounds its own first principles as well as the first principles of other disciplines. In this section, I argue that Aristotle did not see philosophy as related to other sciences in the same way that Plato did, according to this interpretation.

[17]Where do the first principles or starting points of a science come from? Aristotle gives his most extended answer in *Posterior Analytics* II.19, a famous and difficult text in which he describes a process of discovery of first principles that involves both induction and intuition. As the text cited in note 13 above indicates, Aristotle sometimes says that the principles are provided by experience—in this case, the principles of astronomy by astronomical experience.

"prior" and "posterior," "genus" and "species", have application to other sciences. For some such concepts (e.g., genus) are used in other sciences but are not studied by them. The reflections of first philosophy on such concepts will relate this highest science to the other sciences insofar as those sciences make use of the concepts in question. In this way, the science of being is foundational in relation to the other sciences—not as proving that their genera exist and demonstrating their definitions for them, but as reflecting on the notion of a genus and the notion of a definition. The science of being reflects upon those notions which are used in structuring science or knowledge. It thus considers notions that are basic to the structure of all bodies of knowledge, including the science of being itself.[18] First philosophy, or the science of being, is the most universal science because it understands what it is to be any science; it does not know the content of every science (or every possible science), it does not even know the principles of every science (or every possible science). The philosopher, in knowing the first principles, knows everything in a formal sense, in that he or she knows what a science is. And, in contrast with the universality of the science of being, every other science is limited in two ways. The other sciences are parochial in that they are concerned only with a given genus of being, and they are unreflective in that they do not investigate their own foundations.

In light of the material presented in this section, it is necessary to enrich our account of the sort of knowledge achieved by philosophy. Not only does philosophy achieve a systematic understanding of being, but it also knows what constitutes such an understanding (i.e., it has achieved an understanding of understanding and knowledge). Philosophy is thoroughly

---

[18]The most famous example of a first principle of all sciences is the principle of noncontradiction. Aristotle provides a defense of this principle in *Metaphysics* iv. Leaving aside the details of that defense, does this principle provide a counterexample to my claim that first philosophy does not prove or establish the starting point of other sciences? I think it does not, because the principle is a formal principle of a science—like the notion of definition or genus—and Aristotle's reflections upon it are analogous to his reflections on the other formal constituents of a science.

self-reflective. It asks not only about the principles of being, but also about what being is and what a principle is. It achieves not only an understanding of being, but also an understanding of that understanding or knowledge.

In the next section, I illustrate the self-reflective character of the science of being by presenting Aristotle's *aporiai* concerning the principles of being. My discussion of these *aporiai* connects with material presented earlier in this chapter, in that it can serve as an illustration of Aristotle's dialectical method of inquiry. Aristotle's resolution of one of the *aporiai* concerning the nature of principles—namely, the question of whether they are universal or particular—is the central topic of Chapter 5.

4. Aristotle's *Aporiai* Concerning the Principles of Being

The medical example discussed above (§ 2) suggests a clear blueprint for the acquisition of knowledge. One investigates causes—in our example, the cause was the natural constitution of the patient—and builds up a systematic account of the subject at hand (e.g., the medical theory of four natural types of bodily constitution).[19] The doctor posits an area of expertise and, according to a set of principles or causes, tries to organize the facts into a body of knowledge; he or she tries to provide a systematic explanation of the facts. The theoretical scientist (e.g., the mathematician) attempts to demonstrate a large number of theorems concerning a genus of being (namely, the mathematical) based on a small number of accepted principles or starting points.

I said in the last section that the person investigating being does not simply follow this blueprint. Rather, one of his or her roles is to inquire into the nature of the framework itself, and one of the most important issues that arises concerns the principles themselves. Since the science of being *is* a science, it is concerned with the principles, ultimately with the first principles, of being. It is different from other sciences in that it

---

[19]See note 11 above, on Greek medical theory.

does not take the notion of a principle for granted, but asks: What are principles like? How should we conceive of them? The metaphysician asks questions about how to understand the terms used in structuring our understanding of being.

One's first reaction to this development might be to wonder how an investigation into the nature of principles could be possible. After all, the understanding of principles would presumably also be in terms of principles, and so an infinite regress threatens. And it is well known that Aristotle, in other arguments, found an infinite regress unacceptable. Fortunately there are ample illustrations of Aristotle's reflections on this topic in book III of the *Metaphysics*, a book of *aporiai* concerning the principles of being. Aristotle's procedure is to describe different ways of characterizing principles, what favors each, and the consequences that flow from the various ways of thinking about them.

One issue that crops up repeatedly has to do with the nature of the principles of things. Thus, Aristotle asks whether the principles of things are the genera or whether they are the parts present in the things (995b27–29). It is clear, however, that if one were to decide on "genera," other questions remain—in particular, *which* genera, since there are ascending levels of generality. For example, is the principle of men "animal" or "man"? Or should we rather think of the highest genera, "being" and "one," as the principles and elements of beings (998b14ff., 1001a4ff.)? The difficulty concerning the appropriate level of generality of first principles, highest or lowest genus, is explained in terms of degrees of universality: "For if the universals are always more of the nature of principles, it is clear that the highest genera are principles; for they are predicated of all things" (998b17–19). A low genus (e.g., man) is predicated of Socrates, Callias, and the like; a higher genus (e.g., animal) is predicated of more things because it is predicated of all men, all horses, and so on. Hence, the higher genus, animal, is "more universal" than the lower genus, man. The "most universal" genus (e.g., being or one) accordingly, would be predicated of all things.[20] The appeal of the highest

[20]Of course, being is not a genus (see note 15 above). I explain in Chapter

genera to be principles is just that they are principles of every-thing. Whatever is the principle of everything is higher than the more specialized principles. Since the higher principles explain the lower, they explain more. Universal principles ex-plain more things. Truly universal principles would ensure a unified science of wide extent, resting on a small number (per-haps even one) of principles.[21]

Against this line of argument, Aristotle considers an argu-ment from the notion of unity (999a1ff.). As one descends the generic ladder, one arrives eventually at a level, exemplified by man, that is indivisible in form.[22] In contrast, a genus such as animal can be divided into different species of animal. But there are no different species of man. So, man, which is not further divisible, has more unity than animal. And if unity is an important feature of a principle (rather than the property of universality), then the lowest genus or "least universal" will be the principle of things. Unity would appear to be an im-portant feature of an ultimate or first principle; for if a principle were divisible into species by a differentia, then there would be a principle of the principle (namely, the differentia). But, in this case, the first principle would no longer be a *first* principle.

What is at issue here is not whether principles are universal or particular, but what degree of universality or generality is appropriate for principles. There are two appealing criteria that yield different results: universality and unity. In question is at what level to locate the principles of things, assuming that they are generic or universal.

There is another difficulty concerning whether the principles are universal or particular (996a9–10, 1003a5–17). In summary, the dilemma is this: if they are universal, then they will not be substances; if they are particular, then they will not be know-

---

2 that, ultimately, Aristotle does not think that being and unity are predicated *univocally* of all beings. But that conclusion is a part of the work of philosophy.

[21]In the *Critique of Pure Reason* (A654, B682), Kant gives a very similar account of the attraction of the "most universal" principles.

[22]Aristotle here calls species the "lowest genera." It is, of course, possible to question Aristotle's position that there are lowest, indivisible genera, or natural kinds. One might argue, for example, that there is no significant dif-ference between dividing the genus "animal," into its species and dividing the species "man" into its subgroups, e.g., the races.

able (1003a5–17). The contrast in this puzzle is not between lowest and highest genera, but between universal and particular. These terms are defined in book III as follows: "For to say 'one in number' or 'particular' is to say nothing different. For thus we say the particulars are the one in number, but the universal is predicable of them" (999b33–1000a1). Socrates, Callias, and the rest are particulars, and man is a universal predicated of them; so is "animal" or "being" or "one" (the latter two are more universal than the former because they are predicated of every being).

Another, related, puzzle that turns on the contrast between universal and particular arises in connection with knowledge (999a26ff.). If we cannot know an infinite series of particulars, then there must be something that they all share, i.e., a universal. So, if knowledge is possible, there must be universals in addition to particulars. Here, again, the contrast is clearly between particulars and universals, rather than between two levels of universals. This point concerning knowledge bears upon the debate on the nature of principles; it supports universal principles, since it would be very unfortunate if the principles of being were unknowable.

Aristotle calls the puzzle concerning whether the principles are universal or particular "the most difficult of all." Much of what Aristotle says in *Metaphysics* VII–IX concerning substance, definition, and essence is relevant to this issue; and, alternatively, how one interprets those books is partially determined by how (or whether) one thinks Aristotle resolved this puzzle. I discuss this *aporia* in much greater detail in Chapter 5.

5. Analysis of the Question "What Is Substance?"

How is Aristotle's question "What is substance?" related to the science of being? In the next chapter, I will consider Aristotle's argument that the study of being can be unified through a study of substantial being. Before addressing that issue, however, I would like to clarify the distinction I made earlier between the population question and the definitional question with regard to being and substance. Aristotle's investigation of substance, I stated earlier (§ 1), is primarily an investigation of the nature of substantial being, an investigation that is centered on a particular population of substances: namely, sensible substances. In describing Aristotle's project in these terms, I have relied upon a distinction between the population question and the definitional question. The population question seems relatively clear, but what is it to ask for a definition, to ask about the nature or essence of being? What sort of question is it, and what kind of answer would be appropriate?

In order to understand Aristotle's goal in posing the definitional question—the central question guiding his investigation of substance—it is necessary to explain his notion of definition. Aristotle's notion of definition is similar to his notions of knowledge, cause, and principle in that his definitions have features we would not ordinarily associate with the term. First, as the term appears in Aristotle's philosophical and scientific writings, a definition is of a nonlinguistic item (e.g., of a form or a universal). Definitions, in these contexts, do not convey the linguistic meaning of a word. Second, an Aristotelian definition is causal; for Aristotle, one knows what thing is (i.e., its definition) when one knows its cause (*An. Post.* II.2; *Metaph.* VII.17.1041a26–33). These two features of Aristotelian definitions are connected; it would be nonsense to think of the linguistic meaning of a word as the cause of something.

It is helpful to introduce these two features of Aristotelian definitions by glancing at their origins in Plato. That a definition is the appropriate answer to a question of the form "What is F?" is a familiar theme from the early, or Socratic, dialogues of Plato. Indeed, in a summary of his own philosophical tradition, Aristotle attributes the origin of the issue of definitions to Socrates: "Socrates, however, was busying himself about ethical matters and neglecting the world of nature as a whole but seeking the universal in these ethical matters, and he fixed thought for the first time on definitions" (987b1–4). Plato's *Euthyphro* provides an example of the centrality of the definitional question for Socrates' ethical investigations. The question of this dialogue is, "What is piety?" In a very famous passage, Socrates insists that the correct response (i.e., the definition of piety) ought to have two characteristics: (i) it should be of the form (or idea) of piety that makes all pious things pious; (ii) it should provide a standard for judging whether or not a given action is pious (*Euth.* 6d9–e6).

The second characteristic of Socratic definitions, but not the first, is compatible with the familiar idea that a definition ought to give the linguistic meaning of a word. A definition of a word can serve as a standard of correct usage. The first characteristic, however, suggests a very different picture of what a definition is. For it suggests that what gets defined is not a word, but a form or idea—something that makes or causes pious things to be pious. These two ideas—that definitions are of nonlinguistic items and that these nonlinguistic items are causes—are a Platonic contribution to Aristotle's notion of definition. When trying to understand how a form could be a cause, it is important to remember my explanation of Aristotelian causes and how they differ from our notion of a cause. The form or idea is the formal cause of an action being pious, in the sense that it is responsible for the action being pious. The idea of assigning causal responsibility to entities that do not, and cannot, enter into Humean causal relations is a feature common to Platonic and Aristotelian thought.

These features of Aristotelian definition are exemplified by Aristotle's procedure in the chapter of the *Metaphysics* immediately following the chapter in which he proposed the project of defining substance. There Aristotle lists four things that have been thought to be the substance of each thing: essence, universal, genus, and subject or substratum (VII.3.1028b33–36). So, to answer the definitional question concerning substance, Aristotle considers four possible candidates, each a constituent, though not necessarily a material constituent, of individual substances. Which of these four is responsible for, or causes, the thing to be a substance? When Aristotle asks the question "What is substance?" he is asking for the principle or cause of a things's being a substance. He is not asking for the linguistic meaning of the word "substance." Rather, he is asking what it is in or about an entity that causes it to be a substance. Aristotle calls this cause the "cause of being" of the substance. I discuss what Aristotle means by the "cause of being" of a substance, and his claim that the cause of being of a substance is its essence, in Chapter 4.

Chapter 2

BEING AND SUBSTANCE

In the preceding chapter, I said that Aristotle centers his investigation of being upon an investigation of substance, and that he begins with a particular population of substances: namely, sensible substances. In this chapter, I shall examine Aristotle's attempt to unify the study of being around the study of substance.

Metaphysics VII begins with the following statement:

> Being is said in many ways, as we pointed out previously in our book on the number of ways; for in one way it indicates the "what is it" and an individual, and in others it indicates a quality or a quantity or one of the other things that are predicated as these are. While being is said in all these ways, it is obvious that primary among these is the "what is it," the very thing which indicates the substance. [1028a10–15]

Aristotle begins his investigation of being by stating two important yet puzzling doctrines: (i) being is said in many ways and (ii) substantial being is prior to the other kinds of being.

Even though it is not at all clear what these doctrines amount to or why Aristotle thought they were true, it should be evident how they fit into his inquiry into being. For, as I explained in the preceding chapter, Aristotle proposes in place of the traditional question "What is being?" its Aristotelian counter-part—"What is substance?" This substitution might have seemed arbitrary and unmotivated. Why single out one sort or type of being in the investigation of being? The second of the two views helps in this regard; for if substance is prior, i.e., the first or central type or kind of being, then it might make sense to study being by studying substance. Whether or not this is so will depend, to a great extent, on (i) the kind of priority assigned to substance and (ii) the relation between substance and other beings.

In this chapter, I consider the following three questions: What does Aristotle mean when he says, "Being is said in many ways"? Why and how are substances prior? And, given that they are prior to other beings in important respects, does it follow that an understanding of being is constituted by an understanding of substance?

1. Being Is Said in Many Ways

In the text quoted above, Aristotle refers to a discussion of the ways in which being is said in *Metaphysics* v.7, a text in which three major distinctions are drawn: between essential (categorical) being and accidental being; between being as actuality and being as potentiality; and between being as truth and being as falsity.[1] It is clear in the quotation that Aristotle is thinking of essential or categorical being, since he elaborates by referring to different categories of predicates that indicate distinct kinds of beings. Some predicates indicate substance; others qualities, quantities, and so on. In this section, my explanation of what Aristotle means by saying that "being is said in many ways" will be restricted to the distinction between essential being and accidental being.

Aristotle's doctrine of the categories of being is ubiquitous in his writings, including, of course, the treatise titled *Categories*. Nowhere, however, is there any clear evidence con-

---

[1]So, in saying that "being is said in many ways," Aristotle is not simply referring to the doctrine of the categories of being.

cerning the origin or the justification of the list of categories. With regard to the question of origin, one traditional view is that the list resulted from a consideration of questions that one could ask about a person. For example, one could ask "What is it" and the answer, "a man," is a predicate indicating a substance. One could also ask "How big is it?" and the answer might be "five feet," a predicate that refers to a quantity. There are ten categories in all: substance, quantity, qualification, relation, where, when, being-in-a-position, having, doing, being-affected.[2] Because Aristotle's examples of the categories seem to reflect a series of questions asked about a person, the list is traditionally thought to have been generated in that way. But the proposed explanation of how the list was generated does not account for certain apparently arbitrary categories: e.g., being-affected or being-in-a-position. Given an established list of categories, one can imagine it being illustrated through the heuristic device of a series of questions about a person—e.g., What is it? How is it qualified? How big is it? From the fact that Aristotle's examples in the *Categories* suggest questions about a person, however, it does not follow that this was anything more than a heuristic device. Whether or not the list was fashioned in that way, what is really unsatisfying about the "questions about a person" hypothesis is that it does not help us justify the categories. Why ask those questions?

In both the *Categories* and the *Topics*, where the full list of ten categories is given, the presentation is dogmatic.[3] Not only is the origin of the ten categories not discussed, but there is no attempt at a justification of them.[4] That there is a categorical

---

[2]In this list, I have used John Ackrill's translation from his *Aristotle's Categories and De Interpretatione* (Oxford: Clarendon Press, 1963), p. 5. Ackrill's translation and commentary on Aristotle's *Categories* is an excellent introduction to the treatise.

[3]Even though it is not critical to my discussion, it should be remarked that Michael Frede has pointed out important discrepancies between the presentation of the categories in the *Topics* and that in the *Categories* ("Categories in Aristotle," in *Essays in Ancient Philosophy* [Minneapolis: University of Minnesota Press, 1987], pp. 29–48).

[4]To the extent that Aristotle does discuss the features of the various categories, he does not seem to do so for the purpose of justifying the categorical distinctions. In the *Categories*, Aristotle does describe features that are distinc-

distinction between substances (individual horses, human beings, and so on) and qualities ("being pale" or "being educated") might seem intuitively clear. It turns upon the distinction between objects and properties; hence, it seems fundamental and noncontroversial. Other categorical distinctions are not nearly so intuitively appealing, however. Consider, for example, the two categories "affection" and "quality." Why make a categorical distinction between a thing referred to by the predicate "being burned," which indicates an affection, and something referred to by the predicate "being pale," which indicates a quality? Are they not both simply properties? Why make a further categorical distinction between kinds of properties? Why think that they are different kinds of being, or that "being is said differently" in the two cases?

Even if it is difficult to understand why Aristotle made certain categorical distinctions, it is possible to explore another important issue: namely, the question of what kind of classification Aristotle's categories constitute.[5] There are two basic interpretations of Aristotle's categorical distinctions. One way of thinking about Aristotle's categories is to suppose that they represent the ten basic classes or kinds of beings. Any being, according to this view, can be classified under one of ten headings: it is either a substance, or a quality, or a quantity, and so on. According to this view, when Aristotle says that "being is said in many ways," he means that there are different kinds of beings; the categories are simply a list of the ten ultimate kinds of beings. On the other interpretation, Aristotle does not

---

tive of some of the categories. For example, substances are the only beings that can receive contraries and remain numerically the same—Socrates can be short, grow tall, and still remain the same person (see 4a10ff.). Qualities alone provide the basis for judgments of similarity and dissimilarity (11a15–19). There are two reasons for thinking that these remarks are not intended as a justification for the categories. First, not all the categories are discussed in terms of their distinctive features; indeed, the most elusive, the most in need of justification, are omitted. More important, however, even in the discussions we do have, there is no attempt to explain why the distinguishing mark pointed out should ground a categorical difference.

[5]There is a helpful discussion of this question in Joan Kung, "Aristotle on 'Being Is Said in Many Ways,' " *History of Philosophy Quarterly*, 3 (Jan. 1986), 3–18.

think that what it is for a substance to be is the same as what it is for a nonsubstance such as a quality to be. What it is for a substance such as Socrates to be is different from what it is for the quality, "being cultured", to be. On this view, what it means for things to be differs, and the categories represent the ten different ways in which entities are.

Let us explore the differences between the "kind of being" and the "being differs" interpretations of Aristotle's categories by imagining how beings would be sorted according to each. If one views categories as classifying the ultimate kinds of beings, then one considers being or existence as fixed and univocal. One simply sorts objects into kinds, assuming that there is no difference among them in being. Certainly there are differences among the ten kinds, but those differences are not differences in being. This sort of classification is quite familiar. Here is an example: objects could be sorted by color, and each and every object would eventually be placed into one of ten ultimate color kinds. The color of a turquoise and the color of a ruby would presumably fall under two different color kinds, but there would be no difference in what it is for each of them to be a color.

The "being differs" interpretation requires us to imagine another sorting process. In this case, we might imagine ourselves faced with an odd assortment of things—numbers, bodies, thoughts, tools, natural objects, human beings—that differ not simply in the way that the colors differ, but because their being differs: It is at least initially plausible to claim that what it is for a body to be is different from what it is for a thought or a number to be. One might also claim that the being of tools (which can be completely described in functional terms) is different from the being of natural objects, and that both of these differ from the being of humans. However philosophers might want to express and analyze (and analyze away) these differences in being, they are of a different sort from the differences between the colors in my example above. Thoughts and bodies are not simply two kinds of beings; their being differs, as well. In the "being differs" interpretation, one also gets a list that categorizes beings, but *this* list is based on the idea that what it is for different things to be varies.[6]

There are several reasons for thinking that the "being differs" interpretation of Aristotle's categories is correct. For one thing, the "kind of being" interpretation assumes that "being" is a univocal term, and there is very strong evidence that Aristotle did not hold this position.[7] Moreover, there is evidence in the *Metaphysics* and elsewhere of a kind of difference between substances and nonsubstances (entities in the other categories of being) that amounts to a difference in what it is for them to be. One facet of the difference between substances and nonsubstances concerns what I shall call "ontological dependence." The being of nonsubstances intrinsically involves the notion of ontological dependence on a subject, whereas the being of a substance does not involve that notion. So what it is for Socrates (a substance) to be is different from what it is for a quality of Socrates to be, because any quality of Socrates is ontologically dependent upon him but not vice versa.[8] Since there is evidence against the "kinds of being" interpretation and evidence in favor of the "being differs" interpretation, the latter is more plausible.

I illustrated the difference in what it means for things to be by noting the important difference Aristotle finds between the being of substances and the being of nonsubstances—qualities, quantities, and the rest. Of course, the criterion of ontological dependence serves merely to distinguish substantial from nonsubstantial being; hence it does not provide an illustration of the difference in being between two nonsubstantial entities—

[6]Evidence for the "being differs" interpretation can be found in *Metaphysics* v.7. Surely the distinction between being as potentiality/actuality and being as truth/falsity is not tantamount to a distinction between ultimate kinds of being. But these distinctions do fall under the "being is said in many ways" doctrine.

[7]Aristotle denies that "being" is a univocal term when he says that "being is said in many ways" (*Metaph.* 1003a33). He also asserts that being has a different sense for each of the categories (1017a23).

[8]Aristotle expresses this view in *Metaphysics* vii.1; I discuss this text in the next section of the present chapter. A similar view is stated in the *Categories* (2a34–36, 2b3–7).

a quality and an affection. It is difficult to understand why Aristotle thought that what it is for a quality to be differs from what it is for an affection to be. For our purposes, however, this difficulty is not central: our basic interest is in Aristotle's claim that substantial being is prior to nonsubstantial being, and the distinctions between different forms of nonsubstantial being are tangential to that topic. The differences between what it is for a substance to be and what it is for a nonsubstance to be include other characteristics besides ontological independence or dependence and will be elaborated upon later in the present chapter and in Chapter 4.[9]

2. The Unity of the Science of Being

The goal of this chapter is to explain why Aristotle holds that substances are prior to the other forms of being, and to consider to what extent this thesis legitimates studying being by studying substance. Before developing these issues in more detail, however, it is necessary to consider the implications Aristotle's doctrine that "being is said in many ways."

In the preceding chapter (§ 3), I described how the science of being differed from other sciences such as mathematics. And I mentioned, in this connection, Aristotle's doctrine that what it is to be differs for entities in different categories, and that this poses a unique problem for the science of being. Other sciences have a unified subject matter, in that they study a single genus of being and assume both the existence and definition of the genus in question. For first philosophy, or the science of being, however, there are problems with regard to both these assumptions. For Aristotle, as we know, thinks (i) that being is not a genus and (ii) that what it is for the different categories to be varies, i.e., there is no single definition of being applicable across the categories. But if this is so, then there is no science of being, because it cannot meet the criteria any Aristotelian science must meet.

In addressing this difficulty facing the proposed science of

---

[9]In this chapter, see § 3; in Chapter 4, §§ 2 and 3.

being, Aristotle expands upon what he means by the "being is said in many ways" dictum. One option would be to understand the different senses of "being" as referring to entirely unrelated entities. The word "bank" is an example of a word that can refer to two entirely unrelated things—either the side of a river or a place where money is deposited. Once you disambiguate the two senses of the word "bank," it is clear that there is no single kind to be studied by a science of banks. The word "being" could be a homonym like "bank." Or, even though "being" has a number of senses, there could be some sort of unity among the various items to which it refers. Consider, for example, the word "health" and the science of health. The science of health includes the study of many things insofar as they are related to health itself; it studies what produces health, what preserves it, the signs of health, and so on. This science studies a number of diverse things—rashes, foods, forms of exercise—that are unified by their relation to health itself. A rash and a salad are surely as diverse as the side of a river and a place to keep money; the reason that the former can be studied by a single science, but the latter cannot, is that rashes and salads are both related to one thing, health, whereas the two banks have only a name in common.

If "being" indicates different things that are all related to one thing, as in the health example, then, just as there is a science of health, there can be a science of being. In other words, if the various ways that being is said are all related to one thing, then by virtue of that unity there can be a unified science of being. Being, Aristotle says, is said, in relation to one thing, a single nature (*Metaph.* 1003a33–34). All the ways that being is said are related to one principle, which is the being of substances:

> Some things are said to be because they are substances, others because they are affections of substance, others because they are a process toward substance, or destructions or privations or qualities of substance, or productive or generative of substance, or of things which are relative to substance, or negations of one of these things or of substance itself. [1003b6–10]

Aristotle's proposal is that substance plays a role in the science of being analogous to that of health in the science of health: namely, that in relation to which other beings are said to be.[10] There is an important disanalogy between the principle of unity of the science of health and the principle of unity proposed for the science of being. What would be expected, given the model of a science of health that subsumes a wide variety of different health-related items, is a science of being that includes a wide variety of being-related items. In other words, the central principle or nature would be being, and the science of being would study things in relation to that central nature.

But this way of proceeding would lead Aristotle to the verge of holding that, indeed, there is one common way that being is said for all the categories. Aristotle avoids this consequence by proposing that the central nature and principle of being, in relation to which other things are said to be, is substantial being. In so doing, he draws us back from the temptation of extracting a nature of being that is common to all beings. Rather, all beings are said to be by virtue of their relationship to substantial being; and, whatever that may turn out to be, it is not some common nature of being belonging equally to anything that is. In order for this proposal to work in the case of being, however, it is necessary to establish that what it is for nonsubstances to be is dependent upon the being of substances in a nontrivial and systematic way. Also, we need to know what the dependency relationship is, such that it avoids generating common conditions of being for all beings (if we are to avoid contravention of the view that "being is said in many ways").

Aristotle's explanation of how the science of being is possible asserts the dependency of nonsubstances on substances, neither giving grounds for that dependency nor detailing its na-

---

[10]In his important paper "Logic and Metaphysics in Some Earlier Works of Aristotle," in *Articles on Aristotle 3. Metaphysics,* ed. Jonathan Barnes, Malcolm Schofield, and Richard Sorabji (London: Duckworth, 1975), pp. 13–32, G. E. L. Owen first drew attention to Aristotle's proposal for unifying the science of being by means of the notion that the term "being" has a central or "focal" meaning.

ture. He summarizes his proposal as follows: "But everywhere science deals chiefly with that which is primary, and on which the other things depend, and in virtue of which they get their names. If, then, this is substance, it will be of substances that the philosopher must grasp the principles and causes" (1003b16–19). The very possibility of a science of being rests upon the thesis that the being of substances is primary, and that what it is for other things to be is dependent upon what it is for substance to be. In the following section, I consider Aristotle's reasons for holding that substances are prior to the other forms of being. Then (§ 4), I shall explore whether or not this priority justifies the claim that the understanding of being is dependent upon understanding the being of substances.

3. The Priority of Substantial Being

In the opening chapter of *Metaphysics* vii, Aristotle describes the priority of substance as follows:

> Now primary is said in many ways, yet substance is primary in all of them, in definition and in knowledge and in time. For none of the other things predicated is separate, but only substance; and in definition substance is primary (for, necessarily in the definition of each thing, the definition of its substance is present); and we think we know each thing most of all when we know what man or fire is, rather than its quality or quantity or place, since we know each of these whenever we know what the quantity or quality is. [1028a31–b2]

There are three respects in which substance is prior to the other categories of being (quality, quantity, and the rest). Substance is prior in being "separate," whereas the other beings are not. It is also prior in definition: the definitions of the other beings include the definition of substance, but the definition of substance does not include the definition of any other category of being. Finally, it is prior with respect to knowledge, in that knowledge of substance constitutes knowledge in a preferred or special sense.[11]

Aristotle's summary of the threefold priority of substance raises two issues. First, we need to know in greater detail what he means in the three cases and why he holds that substance is prior in each. Second, we need to consider the larger question of whether or not the priority assigned to substance justifies his claim that an inquiry into being should be focused on the study of substance. We shall consider the first issue in the remainder of this section, and the second issue in the next section.

What does Aristotle mean when he says that substance is prior to nonsubstances because it is *separate*? Earlier in the present chapter, while discussing the categories, I said that one important difference between what it is for substances to be and what it is for nonsubstances to be involves the notion of ontological dependence. Every nonsubstance exists in a substance as its subject, but substances are not similarly dependent upon nonsubstances. In the chapter of *Metaphysics* we are now considering, Aristotle uses the term "separate" to express the ontological asymmetry between substances and nonsubstances. That Aristotle uses the term "separate" to express the point that substances are the ontologically basic beings can be gleaned from a text earlier in this chapter, in which he addresses a difficulty that could be formulated for his view that all nonsubstances are said to be in relation to substances:

> For this reason, someone might even raise the puzzle whether each of walking and being healthy and sitting is a being or not, and likewise too for everything else of this sort; for none of them is either *per se*[12] or capable of being separated from substance,

---

[11]There is a scholarly puzzle concerning the relationship between priority in time and Aristotle's explanation of it in terms of substances being separate. For a discussion of this issue, see W. D. Ross, *Aristotle's Metaphysics* (Oxford: Clarendon Press, 1924), vol. 2, pp. 160–161.

[12]Throughout this book I translate Aristotle's phrase "καθ' αὑτὸ" as "*per se*" for convenience. I have found that it is much easier to be consistent and intelligible by using the Latin phrase, rather than the English equivalent "in itself" or "with respect to itself." For a discussion of the meaning of the phrase, see Chapter 4, notes 3 and 8, below. In this context, the term refers to a being

but rather, if anything, it is the walker and the sitter and the
healthy thing that is a being. Now these seem more to be beings
because there is a determinate subject for them (and this is the
substance and the particular), the very thing which is displayed
in this sort of predication. For the good thing or the sitter is not
said without this. [1028a20–29]

In the passage above, Aristotle considers a possible *aporia*
confronting his claim that all nonsubstances are said to be in
relation to substances. For certainly we can refer to nonsubstances by means of expressions such as "walking," as in
"There is some walking." Does "walking" indicate a being or
not? Is walking a being or not? If it is a being, then that would
seem to undercut Aristotle's contention that all nonsubstances
are said to be by reference to substance. If it is not a being, on
the other hand, then how do we explain what is referred to in
the statement "The dog is walking"? To hold that "walking"
and "being healthy" and so on are not beings would tend in
the direction of eliminating all but substantial being. Aristotle's
solution to this *aporia* is to hold that it is not "walking" but a
"walker" that is a being. What he means is that "walking"
cannot exist independently of a subject or substance, something that walks. So, what there really is when there is walking
is a walker. But, Aristotle holds, that there is a walker implies
that there is something that walks, a substance. The phrase
"There is the walker" is less tricky ontologically than "There
is some walking," for it implies a subject or substance that
walks. This statement reveals the correct ontological picture,
since nonsubstances cannot exist separately from a subject or
substance.

The way that Aristotle states his resolution to this *aporia*
might confuse, or sound confused to, contemporary philosophers. For Aristotle distinguishes three things—(i) the walking,
(ii) the walker, and (iii) a substance—whereas philosophers
today might distinguish only two things—(i) the walking and
(ii) the walker, a substance. We might think that a walker is

---

that does not exist in a subject or that exists separately. In denying that certain
phrases refer to *per se* beings, Aristotle is denying that those beings exist
separately.

just a substance and that "the walker" is a definite description that refers to a substance, just as "Socrates" is a name that refers to a substance. If we understand Aristotle's terminology in this way, however, then we might think that when Aristotle says it is "walkers" rather than "walkings" that are beings, he is saying that substances rather than nonsubstances are beings. And this would contradict his own view: namely, that nonsubstances are said to be in relation to substances.

It is clear from the passage quoted above, however, that Aristotle does distinguish between walkers, sitters (and so on) and substances. For he says: "Now these [walkers etc.] seem more to be beings because there is a determinate subject for them (and this is the substance and the particular), the very thing which is displayed in this sort of predication. For the good thing or the sitter is not said without this." There is a clear distinction between beings such as walkers and the thing that underlies them or is their subject (namely, the substance). So, when Aristotle says that walkers and sitters (and so on) are beings, he is not simply saying that substances are beings.

Although it should be clear that Aristotle makes a distinction between an entity like a walker and a substance, it is not yet clear why he makes this distinction. The reason is that, for Aristotle, a walker is an accidental being, a combination of a substance and a nonsubstance, a thing that walks. A substance, on the other hand, is not a compound or accidental being. In *Metaphysics* v.7, in his discussion of the different ways being is said, Aristotle distinguishes between categorical being and accidental being, a distinction that can be exemplified by the distinction between being a human being (a substance) and being a walker (a combination of a substance and an attribute) (1017a7–30). Even though the walker may in fact be a human being (who happens to be walking), Aristotle holds that their being differs—what it is to be a walker differs from what it is to be a human being. At the ontological level, one of them is an accidental being, a compound entity; the other, a substance, is not. And, in the text we have been considering, Aristotle adds two comments about accidental being. The first point is linguistic: the expression "the walker" is preferable to "the walking" because it suggests the correct ontological picture, i.e., a substance underlying the nonsubstance. The second point is ontological: accidental beings cannot exist separately from a subject, i.e., a substance that underlies them.

The upshot of Aristotle's discussion of the *aporia* concerning his view that nonsubstances are said to be in relation to substances is this: there is no walking and there is no walker that exists separately from a subject or substance. On this view, all nonsubstances (properties) exist in substances that are their subjects (substrata). To say that substances are separate is to say that they do not exist in subjects. In this sense, substances are ontologically independent, and nonsubstances are ontologically dependent.[13] According to this understanding of what Aristotle means by the term "separate," substances can be described as the *ontologically basic beings*. The view that substances underlie as subjects all the other categories of being, and that no other beings underlie substances as subjects, suggests by spatial imagery a thesis of ontological foundationalism. Substances are the ontological foundations of what there is; they do not rest on further foundations.

Why did Aristotle think that this picture of ontological foundationalism was true? The answer involves two claims:

(1) All nonsubstances exist in substances as their subjects.

(2) Substances do not themselves exist in anything else as their subjects.

I have already explained the reason that Aristotle holds (1). For it amounts to his view that qualities, quantities, and the rest always exist as the qualities, quantities, etc. of a substance. A quality is a being so long as something, a substance, un-

---

[13]There are other ways of interpreting what Aristotle means by separate substances. A stronger interpretation holds that the notion of separation of substance should be understood as equivalent to what Aristotle elsewhere calls "natural" priority (*Metaph.* 1019a1–4). On this interpretation, when Aristotle says that substances, unlike nonsubstances, are separate, he means that they can exist independently of nonsubstances. For a discussion of the difficulties surrounding this interpretation, see Donald Morrison "Separation in Aristotle's *Metaphysics*," *Oxford Studies in Ancient Philosophy*, 3 (1985), 125–157.

derlies it.[14] Or, to use more contemporary terminology, a necessary condition for the existence of a property is that it is the property of some substance. This claim seems unobjectionable in that it seems obvious that any given instance of a property is always the property of some subject or other. But now a possible difficulty for Aristotle's position arises. For it is one thing to hold that for a property instance to be it must be in a subject, and quite another to hold that properties in general exist only in subjects. Do not some properties, i.e., universals, have independent existence—do they not exist independently of their existence in a subject? The answer to the latter question is "yes," and "no," depending upon how the question is understood. The answer is "yes" if a subject is taken to mean a particular subject. Aristotelian universals do exist independently of their instantiation by any particular subject. The universal "horse" exists independently of the existence of any particular horse. But in another sense of the question, where existence independent of a subject is understood to mean independent of any subject, then the answer is "no." For Aristotle holds that for a universal to exist, there must exist at least one instance of it. And, as just noted, all property instances exist in subjects or substances. If there were no horses, then there would be no universal "horse." The most explicit presentation of these views can be found in the *Categories* (1a20ff., 2a34–b6). I discuss Aristotle's account of universals further in Chapter 5 (§ 2).

In support of claim (2), that substances do not themselves exist in anything else as their subjects, Aristotle would urge us to consider the relationship between a substance and the nonsubstances that inhere in it. Is there some other subject in which the substance itself inheres? Consider a substance such

[14]The way I express the ontological dependency of properties on substances is intended to be neutral on the disputed issue of whether or not Aristotle thought that properties are individuated by their bearers. The two issues are independent of one another; however, if Aristotle did hold that properties are individuated by their bearers, that would be one reason for holding that properties are dependent upon substances. My explanation does not rely upon the individuation thesis. For a discussion of this topic, see G. E. L. Owen, "Inherence," *Phronesis*, 10 (1965), 97–105.

as Socrates: Does Socrates inhere in some other underlying subject? In this case, again, Aristotle's negative answer appears at first sight unobjectionable. After all, substances are simply the bearers of properties; if they were themselves in subjects, then they would be nonsubstances or properties. There is, however, another way of thinking about substances and subjects. For there is the possibility that a substance such as Socrates could be further analyzed so that there is something that underlies him (e.g., his matter). Now the relationship between Socrates and his matter would not parallel exactly the relationship between Socrates and his properties. Socrates does not inhere in his matter as his properties inhere in him. Nonetheless, the claim that Socrates' matter underlies him could be a challenge to Aristotle's general position that substances such as Socrates are the *ontologically basic beings*. Aristotle considers and rejects the position that matter plays an analogous role in relation to Socrates as Socrates plays in relation to his properties; in so doing, Aristotle rejects the view that matter is *ontologically basic*. I consider Aristotle's reasons for this in Chapters 3 and 4.[15]

The second priority Aristotle assigns to substance is priority in definition. He claims that the definition of any nonsubstantial being will include the definition of a substance.[16] Presumably, the reverse is not the case; substances can be defined without mentioning the definition of any nonsubstance. In or-

---

[15]This account is overly simple. Although Aristotle does reject the view that matter is the substance of the composite (*Metaph.* VII.3), and although he does insist that the proper subject of Socrates' properties is Socrates and not his body, Aristotle also refers sometimes to the composite's matter as "material substance." So, even though it is true that matter is not ontologically basic for Aristotle, since it is posterior to both composite and form, this does not prevent him from calling it substance in some contexts (e.g., *Metaph.* VIII.2.1042a26–28).

[16]An alternative interpretation of 1028a35–36 is based on translating the second occurrence of *logos* as "mention" rather than "definition." According to this alternative, the definition of a nonsubstance would require only the mention, rather than the definition, of a substance. Since this interpretation still requires Aristotle to think that the definitions of nonsubstances are incomplete, and since it requires that the meaning of *logos* change in mid-sentence, I do not find it as appealing as the one I have adopted.

der to understand the definitional priority of substance, it is helpful to begin by considering the relationship of the question "What is it?" to Aristotelian definitions and substance.

As I said earlier, Aristotle follows Socrates and Plato in holding that a definition is the appropriate answer to the question "What is it?"[17] And in his initial discussion of the priority of substances, Aristotle claims that a predicate indicating a substance is the appropriate answer to that same question (1027b13–15). Indeed, he even refers to the category of substance as the "what is it":

> But though being is said in so many ways as this, it is evident that primary among these is the "what is it," the very thing which indicates substance (for when we say of what quality a thing is, we say that it is good or bad, not that it is three cubits or a man; but when we say what it is, we say not pale or hot but a man or a god. [1028a13–18]

If the definition is the appropriate answer to the question "What is it?" and if the question "What is it?" is appropriately answered by a term indicating the substance, then the definition will be the definition of the substance. Following this line of thought, then, will lead to the conclusion that definitions will be restricted to substances. This position is considered in some detail by Aristotle in chapters 4 and 5 of book VII, and I shall have more to say about it in Chapter 4 (§ 2) of the present book.

It is clear, however, that at this point Aristotle makes a weaker claim in holding that substances are prior in definition to nonsubstances. For he does not say that nonsubstances cannot be defined but, rather, that their definitions must include the definitions of substance. And now we are not at all sure how to understand this priority claim; nor do we know why Aristotle thought it was true.

Here is a possible explanation of Aristotle's reasoning. Let us suppose, as Aristotle does, that no nonsubstance is capable

---

[17]Aristotle says that Socrates pioneered the search for definitions in philosophy (*Metaph.* I.6 and XIII.9).

of existence separate from substance. Now, consider one of Aristotle's examples, the quality "being good." In defining that quality, we ask the question "What is it?" But because what we are defining is a quality, a nonsubstance, we know that it inheres in a substance. Whenever we are defining a nonsubstance, we are always defining a nonsubstance-in-a-substance; there are no independently existing nonsubstances, and so there are none to be defined. Suppose, for example, we are defining the quality "being good"; on Aristotle's view, what we are really defining is good-in-man or good-in-a-god.[18] But to spell out the full definition of good-in-a-man or good-in-a-god requires inclusion of the definitions of man and god, respectively. Otherwise, we will have provided only a partial definition. But the definitions of man and god would not include the definitions of any nonsubstances, for men and gods are capable of independent existence.

The example I have just considered suggests two distinct explanations of the claim that substances are prior in definition. The first, which is a function of our particular example, is that the definitions of good vary in relation to the substances. For it is plausible to think that what it is for a man to be good is different from what it is for a god to be good. According to this account, the *content* of the definition of the nonsubstance is held to vary, perhaps significantly, depending upon the identity of the substance. But this explanation of priority in definition, based on the idea that the nature of the substance will affect the *content* of the definition of the nonsubstances, does not apply to all cases. For instance, as I explain below, it does not seem to apply to the definition of quantities. Because this explanation is plausible in only a very restricted number of cases, there must be some other reason why Aristotle thinks that in the definition of every nonsubstance, the definition of the substance must be present.

The second explanation turns on the notion of the *complete-*

---

[18]In this discussion of priority in definition, the objects of Aristotelian definitions do not appear in quotation marks to indicate a point made earlier (in Chapter 1, § 5) that Aristotle's real definitions are of things and not words.

ness of the definition, rather than on the determination of its content. Consider another of Aristotle's examples of a nonsubstance, the quantity three-cubits. A cubit is equal to the length from the elbow to the tip of the middle finger. According to Aristotle's claim about the priority of definition, the definition of three-cubits includes the definition of a substance. But this cannot be because in every case the definition of three-cubits would vary as the identity of the substance varies, for that seems simply to be false. The definition of three cubits does not vary depending upon whether it is a goddess or a mortal who has hair of that length. For this reason, it is more plausible to understand the priority-of-definition claim as concerning the completeness of the definition, rather than its content, although in some cases (the example in the preceding paragraph) the completion of the definition (i.e., the inclusion of the definition of the substance) will affect the content as well.

Why is the definition of three-cubits as, say, "three times the length from the elbow to the tip of the middle finger" incomplete? Because three-cubits is the quantity of a substance (all nonsubstances inhere in substances), and the complete articulation of its definition—the statement that says what it *is*—must therefore include the definition of the substance in which it inheres. What is being defined is three-cubits-in-a-substance, not just three-cubits (on Aristotle's view, there is no such entity to be defined). But if one is defining three-cubits-in-a-substance, one's definition will be incomplete unless one includes a statement of what the substance is. If one leaves out the definition of the substance, one will not have defined one constituent of a compound entity. One will have only a partial definition of the being in question.

In order to understand Aristotle's perspective, it is helpful to recall two features of Aristotelian definitions. First, such definitions are real: they are not meant to convey the linguistic meaning of a term; they are meant to explain what the thing in question is. Indeed, in the preceding discussion, in order to signal the important difference between Aristotelian *real* definitions (that are of things and not words) and our ordinary notion of *linguistic* definitions (that are of words and not things), I did not place the object of definition in quotation marks as would be appropriate for the object of a linguistic definition, i.e., a word. So, it would be a serious misunderstanding of Aristotle's point to think that he has formulated a bizarre requirement for specifying the linguistic meaning of certain words (i.e., those used to refer to nonsubstances). Second, Aristotelian definitions are causal: if one wants to say what something is, one should say *why* it is. Now, Aristotle thinks that every nonsubstance exists because of a substance in which it inheres (1028a25–28). There is the walking only insofar as there is the walker, and there is the walker only insofar as there is a substance that walks. So, in order to say what a nonsubstance is, in order to explain it, one would have to specify the substance in which it inheres.

The third priority Aristotle assigns to substances is priority in knowledge: "and we think we know each thing most of all when we know what man or fire is, rather than its quality or quantity or place, since we know each of these whenever we know what the quantity or quality is"(1028a36–b2). Here Aristotle draws out the implications of the priority of substances in definition. In the first place, the definition of the substance is central to knowing the thing. It is much more important to know what a man is than to know what are the various nonsubstances that inhere in man. If one knows what a man is, one knows more about Socrates than one knows from Socrates' various properties. Knowledge of substance is more informative than knowledge of nonsubstance.

It might be objected that this is obviously true if what one is knowing is a substance, such as Socrates, but not so obviously true if one is knowing a nonsubstance. Surely, knowledge of substance is not prior and more informative if what one is knowing is a quantity or a quality. In order to see why Aristotle thinks that, even in these cases, knowledge of substance has a special status and priority, we need to remember the priority of substance for definition. When do we know in the fullest sense a quantity or a quality? We know it, Aristotle says, when we know what the quantity or quality is. There are other things we could know about the quantity (e.g., where it is), but we know the quantity most fully when we know its definition. But to know the definition of a quantity involves knowing the definition of a substance. So, in the case of the fullest knowledge of nonsubstances, the knowledge of substance plays a central role. If knowing the definition constitutes knowledge in the fullest sense, and if the definition of nonsubstances includes the definition of substances, then even the fullest knowledge of nonsubstances will depend upon the knowledge of substances. But, because the definitions of substance do not include the definitions of nonsubstances, complete knowledge of substances will not depend upon the knowledge of nonsubstances. Hence, substances are prior to nonsubstances with respect to knowledge.

4. The Priority of Substance and the Science of Being

In the preceding section, I discussed the three ways in which substance is prior to the other categories of being. In this section, I shall explain how the three priorities are related to one another, and I shall consider to what extent they justify Aristotle's proposal to focus the study of being on the study of substantial being.

Substance is primary in three ways: it is prior to nonsubstances in being separate, in definition, and in knowledge. Is there a systematic connection between these priorities of substance, or is each entirely independent of the other? According to the interpretation I have proposed for the three priorities, they are related to one another; priority in definition and priority in knowledge both depend ultimately on Aristotle's claim that substance is separate and that nonsubstances are not capable of separate existence. In other words, on my interpretation, the priority in definition and knowledge attributed to substance depends upon the claim that substances are the ontologically basic beings.

To see these connections, we can begin by considering priority in definition and knowledge. According to my explanation of priority in knowledge, substances are prior even for the knowledge of nonsubstances because the definitions of non-substances must include the definition of substance. To answer the question "What is it?" with regard to a nonsubstance requires that one answer the same question with regard to a substance. Since the definition of any being provides knowledge of it in the fullest sense, any instance of knowledge in the fullest sense will involve knowledge of the definition of a substance. If nonsubstances could be defined *without* including the definition of substance, then we could have full knowledge of nonsubstances quite independently of knowledge of substance, and there would be cases of knowledge in the fullest sense in which knowledge of substance would not be needed. If this were so, however, there would be no reason to think that knowledge of substance is prior to knowledge of other things quite generally.

Now, consider the explanation I offered for Aristotle's claim that substances are prior in definition. Substances are prior in definition because the definition of any nonsubstance must include the definition of a substance. If it does not, then the definition is incomplete. It will be incomplete because all non-substances inhere in substance; a substance figures in the explanation of their being. And since Aristotelian definitions are explanatory, a substance figures in nonsubstance definitions. In this way we can trace priority in knowledge back to priority in definition, and priority in definition back to the notion that substances are separate and nonsubstances are not capable of separate existence.

The priority of substance in definition and knowledge does not simply *follow* from the fact that substances are ontologically basic. For these two priorities also involve distinctive views about the nature of definition and knowledge, respectively. Priority in definition relies upon the view that definition is an answer to the question "What is it?" and does not merely give the linguistic meaning of a word. Priority in knowledge, in turn, relies upon the claim that knowledge in the fullest sense is knowledge of definitions. These views would not have struck Aristotle's audience as idiosyncratic, as they might strike us.

For, as I pointed out above, they are found elsewhere in contemporary Greek philosophical thought (e.g., in Plato).[19] Aristotle is drawing upon familiar notions of definition and knowledge in establishing the priority of substance. To be precise, he is drawing out the logical consequences, with regard to familiar notions of definition and knowledge, of his view that substances are the basic subjects.

To what extent does the threefold priority of substance justify Aristotle's proposal to study being by studying substance? In Aristotle's words, quoted earlier: "But everywhere science deals chiefly with that which is primary, and on which other things depend, and in virtue of which they get their names. If, then, this is substance, it will be of substances that the philosopher must grasp the principles and causes"(1003a16–19). The first priority is simply the claim that the primary being is substance, in the sense that all nonsubstances depend upon substance for their being; thus, nonsubstances are not capable of existing in separation from substances. The other two priorities are extremely important, however, for justifying the claim that the science of being will consist in grasping the principles and causes of substance.

The spelling-out of the priority of substance in definition and knowledge is necessary if we are to connect the notion that substance is primary being with the notion that a science of being can be achieved through the study of substance. It needed to be explained how it is that in studying substance one is at the same time studying something systematically basic to understanding nonsubstances. If, as Aristotle claims, the definition and knowledge of nonsubstances include the definition and knowledge of substances, then by studying and knowing substance through its principles and causes, one will also attain knowledge necessary for the understanding of nonsubstances.

So far, we have seen why Aristotle thinks that in grasping

[19]That the question "What is it?" is intended to extract a definition from Socrates' interlocutors is an omnipresent assumption in Plato's earlier dialogues. That knowledge of definitions is the central case of knowledge is stated in the opening lines of the *Meno*.

the principles and causes of substances we will come to understand something central to understanding nonsubstances. It is still not clear, however, whether or not Aristotle's science of being is restricted to the study of the principles and causes of substances, as suggested by the text just quoted, or whether the science of being begins with the principles and causes of substances but then goes on to study the principles and causes of nonsubstances, as well. When Aristotle says that the philosopher must grasp the principles and causes of substance, does he mean that the philosopher does this first, and then goes on to study nonsubstance? Or does he restrict the science of being to the study of the principles and causes of substance?

At first glance, the second alternative—that the science of being is restricted to an inquiry into the principles and causes of substances—suggests that the science of being is not a universal science. For how can a science restricted to the study of substance be a science of being *qua* being? Surely the science of being *qua* being must also study the principles and causes of nonsubstances. If understanding substance is central to understanding other beings, certainly it makes sense to begin with substance; but, as yet, there does not seem to be any reason to restrict the science of being to ousiology (i.e., the science of substance).

On the other hand, the above text does seem to say that the science of being should inquire into the principles and causes of substances alone. How can we understand this restriction? In the first place, as we saw in § 2 above, Aristotle thinks that substances are the principles and causes of nonsubstances. More precisely, substances are the principles or causes of being of nonsubstances. This does not mean that nonsubstances do not have other kinds of principles and causes—surely they do. The science of chromatics has the task of formulating the principles and causes of colors; the science of measurement has the same task with respect to quantities. But it does mean that *with regard to their being* nonsubstances do not have any other principles or causes. To study substances is to study, among other things, the principles and causes of being of nonsubstances. Because Aristotle thinks, as I explained in Chapter 1, that science is the grasp of principles and causes, then once it is shown that substance is the cause of being for nonsubstance, there is no reason for the science of being to concern itself further with nonsubstance. The central question guiding the science of being is simply this: What are the principles and causes of substance?

In closing, I think it important to note the scope of the argument presented in this chapter and to explain how it is broadened in later chapters. On my interpretation, Aristotle holds that substances are prior to nonsubstances in three ways. But, what is included under the heading "nonsubstances"? As far as this chapter goes, the nonsubstances in question are the entities in the other categories of being, e.g., attributes such as quantities and qualities. I argue later, however, that Aristotle broadens his position to include the priority of substances (form and composite) in relation to universals (including sortals such as "man" or "horse") and in relation to matter. In Chapter 5, § 2, I consider Aristotle's arguments to the conclusion that universals are nonsubstances in a context in which the priority of substances over nonsubstances (in this case universals) is clearly at issue (*Metaph.* XIII.10.1086b37–1087a4). And, in Chapter 4, § 5, I argue that Aristotle holds that substance is prior in being and definition to matter.[20]

[20]As I remarked above in note 15, Aristotle does call matter "substance" in certain contexts, so one cannot simply call matter "nonsubstance", as one can attributes and universals. On the other hand, it is accurate to group matter with attributes and universals in relation to the priority which Aristotle holds that substances (Form and composite) have to all three.

Chapter 3

THE METAPHYSICAL STRUCTURE OF SENSIBLE SUBSTANCES

Aristotle argues in *Metaphysics* VII.1 that all nonsubstances inhere in substances; substances are the ontologically basic subjects. In the following chapter, Aristotle presents a lengthy list of candidates for substantial being, canvassing the opinions of philosophers and common sense—earth, air, fire, water, Platonic Forms, numbers, and so on (1028b8–27). This list represents possible answers to the population question ("Is *x* a substance?"). I said in Chapter 1 that Aristotle thinks there is a prior question to be addressed: namely, the definitional question ("What is substance?"). Once one knows what substance is, one has a means for deciding the population question. Aristotle thinks that individuals such as Socrates—what he calls "sensible substances"—are judged by many to be substances, and so he proposes to investigate the definition question by examining these uncontroversial examples. Aristotle himself is among those who think that individual, sensible substances are clear examples of substances; indeed, in the *Categories*, they are the primary substances.[1]

[1] In the *Categories*, Aristotle distinguishes between primary and secondary substances (3b10ff.). An individual substance such as Socrates is an example of a primary substance, and the species "human being" is an example of a secondary substance.

Sensible substances, however, are composites of form and matter; a human being, for example, is a composite of the appropriate kind of soul and the appropriate kind of body. Aristotle often refers to them as "composites" or "composite substances."[2] The composite, form, and matter are first mentioned in book VII, chapter 2, in connection with the notion that substances are the ontologically basic beings, the basic subjects. If we consider a sensible substance (e.g., a horse), it is not clear exactly in what the nonsubstances inhere. Is the subject of inherence the horse, i.e., the composite? Is it the horse's matter? Or is it the horse's form? Before we pursue this question further, however, it is necessary to introduce and clarify Aristotle's notions of matter and form.

As the problem we have just been considering suggests, Aristotle brings to his reflections on substance in the *Metaphysics* a number of concepts that he assumes in the discussion; he is not particularly concerned to introduce or justify these concepts. The notions of form and matter, which Aristotle uses repeatedly in his investigation of sensible substance, are themselves not given any lengthy introduction. What, exactly, does Aristotle mean by these concepts? Further, Aristotle does not defend at any length his analysis of the structure of sensible substances in terms of two principles—matter and form. As we have seen, one of Aristotle's main problems in *Metaphysics* VII–VIII is to determine the principles and causes of sensible or composite substances. But, one might ask, why accept the matter/form (or hylomorphic) analysis of composite substances, rather than some alternative understanding of their nature? And to an-

---

[2]In what follows, I refer to the same entities as material or sensible or composite substances. Individual substances such as Socrates are material substances because they are composites of form and matter; Aristotle also countenances immaterial substances. That Aristotle refers alternately to the very same class of beings (exemplified by individual plants and animals) as sensible substances or composite substances can be seen in a passage in *Metaphysics* VII.15. In this passage, Aristotle begins by pointing out that composite substances are generated and perish (1039b20–22). He then says that *for that reason* there is no definition of individual sensible substances (1039b27–30).

swer *that* question, we need first understand what Aristotle means by the concepts "form" and "matter." In order to address these two issues, we shall have to look to texts other than the *Metaphysics* itself.[3]

1. Nature as Form and Nature as Matter: The *Physics*

In *Metaphysics* v.4, a chapter devoted to the discussion of the various meanings of the term "nature," Aristotle mentions both matter and form (1014b26–1015a5). The sense in which matter and form are both natures is explained in the *Physics*. Aristotle conceives of his project in the *Physics* as investigating nature systematically, by investigating its "primary causes and principles" (184a10–16). I said in Chapter 1 that, for Aristotle, understanding a phenomenon or subject matter always involves a grasp of the principles and causes that are responsible for it. The notions of matter and form play a minor role in his analysis of change in *Physics* I.7 and are at the heart of Aristotle's discussion of the causes of the generation and corruption of natural beings in *Physics* II. We can begin to understand Aristotle's concepts of matter and form by considering these two contexts.

One natural phenomenon, whose correct principles were hotly disputed in Aristotle's philosophical milieu, is change. Imagine a leaf turning from green to red. How are we to understand this occurrence? If we think of the red leaf as just popping into existence from nothing at all, then it seems inexplicable. When a change occurs, something must persist through it. But if the changing thing somehow existed all along, then the phenomenon of change itself seems

---

[3]This claim requires modification, for Aristotle makes it clear that the discussion of form in the *Physics* is limited, and that a full discussion of form is the work of first philosophy (192a35–b1). Moreover, Aristotle elaborates upon the notions of form and formal cause in the *Metaphysics*, in his discussions of definitions and essence.

to have evaporated.[4] Aristotle's purpose in *Physics* i.7 is to explain the phenomenon of change by the use of principles that enable his account to avoid the following dilemma: (i) change occurs from nothing, or (ii) no change occurs at all. His account preserves and reconciles our double intuition concerning change: namely, that in every change something changes and something persists. He uses the notion of "opposites" to explain what changes (in our example, the opposits are the colors green and red), and he employs the notion of a "subject" or "underlying thing" to explain what persists (in our example, the leaf).

In other cases—namely, changes that are not simply changes in property, but are generations or corruptions of substances (what he calls "coming to be absolutely")—Aristotle follows the same schema of opposites and substratum:

> Things are said to come to be in many ways, and some things are said not to come to be, but to come to be something, while only substances are said to come to be absolutely. In the case of other things it is plain that there must be something underlying which is the thing that comes to be—when a quantity, quality, relation, [time] or place comes to be, it is of an underlying thing, since it is only substances which are not said of another underlying thing and all other things are [said] of substances. But that substances, too, and whatever things are absolutely, come to be out of something underlying, will, if you look attentively, become plain. There is always something which underlies, out of which the thing comes to be, as plants and animals come to be out of seed. [190a31–b5][5]

In the case of the generation of substances, the notion of form is employed in Aristotle's specification of the opposites, and the notion of matter in his conception of the underlying thing or subject:

[4]For an interesting and extensive discussion of the philosophical difficulties surrounding the topic of change, see Sarah Waterlow, *Nature, Change, and Agency in Aristotle's Physics* (Oxford: Oxford University Press, 1982). My understanding of the *Physics* has been influenced by Waterlow's book.

[5]My translations of the *Physics* are based on W. Charlton's excellent translation: *Aristotle's Physics: Books I and II* (Oxford: Clarendon Press, 1970).

> As for the underlying nature, it must be grasped by analogy. As bronze stands to a statue, or wood to a bed, or [the matter and] the formless before it acquires a form to anything else which has a definite form, so this stands to a substance and an individual and a being. [1917–12]

As in his analysis of change in general, the underlying thing or substratum in the generation of substances is a single thing, the unformed matter, which has two aspects distinguishable in definition: the matter and the lack of form (190b23–28). But the specification of the content of the notion "lack of form," or "formless," must be done in relation to a substance having form. Hence the explanation by instances given in the quotation above. Aristotle's examples give us a rough idea of what matter is in the context of substantial generation—the bronze from which a statue is made and the wood from which a bed is made. In each case, the matter is the persisting substratum of the change.

Concrete examples of form are harder to extract from this chapter. Aristotle says: "As for the form, it is one; it is the arrangement, or the knowledge of music or some other thing predicated in this way" (190b 27–29). From this statement, it is clear that Aristotle, in this context, indifferently applies the term "form" to the property acquired in the change from being an unmusical person to becoming a musical one, as well as to the "arrangement" of matter that constitutes the generation of a substance. This is not surprising, however, because Aristotle's primary concern in *Physics* I.7 is to isolate the general principles of coming to be, which he then applies (making the appropriate changes in terminology) to the case of substantial generation. The application of the principles to the case of substantial change is eased by Aristotle's willingness to treat substantial form and the properties acquired in change alike as positive contraries, just as he treats the proximate matter of a substantial change and the substance acquiring a property alike as subjects, or things underlying the change.

More can be gleaned about Aristotle's notions of form and matter as they are used in the analysis of composite substances from his discussion of natural beings in *Physics* II. For composite substances are included in the set of natural beings: "Some things are due to nature; for others there are other causes. Of the former sort are animals and their parts, plants, and simple bodies such as earth, fire, air, and water—for we say that these and things like them are due to nature" (192b9–12). At first sight, this list might seem to be quite heterogeneous. What feature or features do these beings have in common? Aristotle's response is that they have in themselves a source or principle of change and rest. The term "nature" refers to the inner source, or cause, of change and rest possessed by these beings; they are called "natural beings" by virtue of possessing natures. Aristotle contrasts natural beings with artifacts, which, apart from the nature of the matter that composes them, lack inner principles of change and rest (192b13–23).

Aristotle proceeds in this chapter to describe two ways of conceiving of nature: one can think of a being's nature as its matter or as its form. Is an animal's nature its matter—its body or bodily parts—or its form—its soul or principle of life? Presently we shall consider Aristotle's discussion of these two options in some detail, as it helps to clarify his notions of matter and form. Before doing so, however, a preliminary issue demands our attention. For it is not at all clear what Aristotle means by "an inner principle of motion and rest"; consequently, it is not at all clear how natural beings differ from nonnatural beings (e.g., artifacts). Aristotle thinks it is obvious that there are natural beings and that no proof could be more self-evident than this obvious fact (193a2–8). That may be true, but we can still wonder about natural beings and how they differ from artifacts. On reflection, is there is any reason to distinguish between animals, on the one hand, and tables, on the other, with regard to the principle(s) governing their behavior?

Two issues require clarification. First, how are we to understand Aristotle's position that some beings (e.g., animals) have natures, or inner principles of motion and rest, and others (e.g., artifacts) do not have natures? Second, how are we to understand the "inner principle" assigned to natural beings in terms of its causal efficacy? Do natual beings move and rest, grow and change owing entirely to an internal cause or principle? Are other causes involved? And, if so, what contribution does the internal principle make to the natural being's behavior?[6]

In his introduction of the concept of nature, before he describes the two candidates for being the natures of natural beings (i.e., form and matter), Aristotle says very little to explain either the causal efficacy of the inner principle or the contrast between natural beings and artifacts.[7] He does make one statement, however, that is germane to both issues and deserves careful scrutiny. Contrasting artifacts with natural beings, Aristotle says:

> Similarly with other things which are made. They none of them have in themselves the source of their making, but in some cases, such as that of a house or anything else made by human hands, the source is in something else and external, whilst in others the source is in the thing, but not in the thing *per se*, i.e., when a thing comes to be a cause to itself *per accidens*. [192b27–33]

[6]There is the widest possible range of scholarly opinion on the issue of the causal role of a being's nature, which Aristotle later identifies with form rather than with matter. One extreme is illustrated by Charlton, who interprets Aristotle as holding merely that under one description all the being's motions can be explained mechanistically, while under another (intentional) description they cannot be so explained (*Aristotle's Physics*, pp. 92–93). One shortcoming of this explanation of the causal role of the inner principle is that it does not provide any reason for discriminating, as Aristotle does, between natural beings such as animals and artifacts. For we can also use an intentional idiom to describe the behavior of artifacts; thus, Charlton's account provides no basis for Aristotle's distinction between natural beings and artifacts. The other extreme is exemplified by Waterlow, who interprets the causal role of the inner principle strongly, in that she holds that natural beings are self-sufficient to determine the pattern of their typical changes (*Nature, Change, and Agency*, p. 38). I believe that Waterlow's position is correct; see, for example, *Physics* 199a8–13.

[7]Because Aristotle does not discuss the distinction between natural beings and artifacts at any length, it might be tempting to explain that distinction in terms of Aristotle's later arguments in favor of formal/final causes over material causes. The idea is that, in the case of artifacts, teleology is dispensable because they can be given a purely material explanation. But Aristotle does not make this distinction later, and he seems to think that mention of the end, or final cause, is required in the explanation of artifacts and natural beings alike.

Let us ignore the complication Aristotle introduces in the latter part of this passage.[8] In the first part, his point appears to be clear, seeming to address both the question of causal efficacy and the question of the basis for a distinction between natural beings and artifacts (e.g., between animals and houses). Let us consider the latter issue first. Natural beings (e.g., animals), Aristotle says, have an internal source or principle of their own generation, whereas artifacts are made by an external agent.

At first glance, this point of contrast seems wrong, even within Aristotle's own system of thought. For, according to Aristotle, the generation of an animal is *not* accomplished by the animal itself. As I said in the first chapter (§ 2), Aristotle explains the generation of an animal by the four causes, and he says that the form comes from the male parent and the matter from the female parent. In many places, moreover, Aristotle says that the efficient cause of the generation of an animal is the male parent. The causal factors that Aristotle standardly mentions—form, matter, efficient cause—all originate in individuals other than the one being generated, so it is difficult to see how natural beings have an inner source of their own generation. Further, Aristotle often emphasizes the similarity between the production of an artifact and the generation of a natural being. Indeed, he emphasizes or relies upon the similarity between the two cases so frequently that one common criticism of Aristotle's account of the workings of nature is that he illegitimately and unreflectively employs principles applicable to artifacts in his analysis of nature.[9]

Careful study of Aristotle's account of the generation of animals, however, reveals an important difference between the

---

[8]The complication concerns the way in which the source is in natural beings. It is not accidentally in the thing, as in the case of a doctor who heals himself. In this case, the source of motion is only accidentally in the patient, since the patient happens to be a doctor (*Physics* 192b20–27).

[9]This passage from the *Generation of Animals* is typical of Aristotle's tendency to treat nature and art as parallel: "Everything produced naturally or by an art is produced by a thing existing actually out of what is potentially of that sort" (734b21–22).

natural event and the production of an artifact. In his account of the generation of one sort of natural being (i.e., animals), Aristotle explains that the semen contributed by the male parent contains movements that convey soul to the matter provided by the female. Organ formation proceeds serially, as the matter is shaped up into the successive organs by the movements in the semen (*Gen. An.* 734b9ff.). Aristotle compares the production of artifacts with natural generation and insists that, in both sorts of production, the key causal element is form, rather than the mechanistic causes at work in the matter. In this connection, he mentions a difference between the two cases that is relevant to the distinction made between natural and nonnatural beings in *Physics* II.1:

> It is the same with things produced according to an art. Heat and cold make the iron hard and soft, but the *sword* is made by the instrument's movement which contains a definition belonging to the art. For the art is source and form of the product, but in another thing; but the movement of nature is in the thing itself, being derived from another nature which contains the form actualized. [*Gen. An.* 734b30–735a4][10]

Natural and artificial production are similiar in that form is identified as the source of the artifact and of the natural being. They differ in that the form involved in the creation of an artifact is in another being (i.e., the art is in the mind of the creator), whereas the form involved in natural production,

---

[10]In *Meteorology* IV.12, Aristotle again denies that simply the mechanistic causes at work in matter could account for the production of an animal's organic parts: "Now heat and cold and the motions they set up as the bodies are solidified by the hot and the cold are sufficient to form all such parts as are the homogeneous bodies, flesh, bone, hair, sinew, and the rest. For they are all of them differentiated by the various qualities enumerated above, tension, ductility, fragmentability, hardness, softness, and the rest of them: all of which are derived from the hot and the cold and the mixture of their motions. But no one would go so far as to consider them sufficient in the case of the nonhomogeneous parts (such as the head, the hand, or the foot) which the homogeneous parts go to make up. Cold and heat and their motion would be admitted to account for the formation of copper or silver, but not for that of a saw, a bowl, or a box. So here, save that in the examples given, the cause is art, but in the nonhomogeneous bodies nature or some other cause"(390b3–14).

even though it originates in another individual, guides the development of the embryo from within. A potter molds and shapes the clay according to a form that is in his or her mind; the embryo molds and shapes itself according to its form. In the latter case, there is no external causal agent that brings the offspring to full development. It is a natural being because it has an inner principle of motion, or nature, that directs its development.

Generation is just one sort of motion, and the natures of natural beings are principles of their motions in general. We have just seen the sense in which natural beings and artifacts are contrasted by Aristotle on the point of self-generation. We might ask why Aristotle cites self-generation as his illustration of the operation of the inner principle. It is reasonable to suppose that he chose self-generation because it provides both a vivid illustration of the inner principle's causal power and a sharp point of contrast between natural beings and artifacts. Whatever one's view might be on the details of the process of generation, it is clear that every change (related to the production of an artifact) that the material undergoes is initiated at each stage by an external agent, and it is equally clear that the same level of external guidance does not govern the development of plants and animals.

To show the clarity of the generation example, we can contrast this illustration of the operation of the "inner principle" with an illustration based on the consideration of mature examples of an artifact and a natural being. To borrow an example from W. Charlton, if we think of a washing machine, it seems as though we can attribute its behavior to its nature, exactly as we can attribute the behavior of a dog to its nature:

> Nor would it help Aristotle to concentrate on the behaviour of completed artifacts and mature living things, for if a dog gives chase when it sees a rabbit because it is a dog, why not say that my washing machine washes and spin-dries my shirts when I press the programme-button C because it is a washing machine,

i.e., has the internal structure and disposition of parts of a washing machine.[11]

The process of generation of a natural being and the production of an artifact, unlike the behavior of mature or completed specimens, marks a clear contrast between the two sorts of beings. Even though we can attribute some of the motions of a complicated machine such as a washing machine, or an automaton of the sort with which Aristotle might have been familiar, to an inner rather than an external origin (i.e., the structure of the artifact), they still differ from animals and plants with regard to self-generation. Self-generation, then, is a particularly striking example of the effects of natures on the behavior of natural beings; hence it is a clear example of the working of the inner principle that distinguishes natural beings from non-natural beings.[12]

In the previous paragraphs, I have said that the distinction between the principle governing natural and nonnatural generation—namely, that one is an internal and the other an external principle—provides a vivid and accessible illustration of the basis for Aristotle's distinction between natural and nonnatural beings. At the same time, it provides an example of the causal efficacy of the inner principle. But how are we meant to understand our example in connection with this issue? What is the extent of the causal efficacy of the inner principle in the case of the generation of an animal?

Since Aristotle treats them as parallel, it might be helpful

---

[11]Charlton, *Aristotle's Physics*, p. 89.

[12]According to Waterlow, the difference in genetic process between natural beings and artifacts is only an empirical difference and, therefore, is inadequate to secure the distinction: "Of course the genetic process is empirically different in each case, but *what* comes into being in each case is a system of essentially the same logical type, demanding in the end the same type of explanation for its behaviour and characteristics" (*Nature, Change, and Agency*, p. 52). I disagree. I do not see why the difference between self-generated and other-generated entities is merely an empirical difference. True, at the most general level, Aristotle explains both sorts of entities by the four causes. But this does not mean that the difference between having an internal or external, formal /final / efficient cause is merely empirical.

to consider this issue by comparing the causal efficacy of the external principle in artificial generation with the causal efficacy of the internal principle in nature. In the process of production of an artifact, the artist is the efficient cause of the production by enforming some appropriate matter through motions that express the form or art the artist has in mind. It is only because the artist possesses the art, and is acting in accordance with it, that he or she is the efficient cause of the artifact. Similarly, in the case of the development of the animal embryo, the motions in the semen (which comes from the male parent) act directly on the matter; the motions are the efficient cause of the animal only because they are motions that express its form.[13] It seems clear from Aristotle's discussion in *Generation of Animals* that the internal principle that is responsible for the self-generation of animals has the causal power to accomplish this goal in the appropriate circumstances; i.e., initially matter and, later, nutrition are required from the female. Analogously, the artist has the causal power to create an artifact in suitable circumstances—when he or she has available the appro-

---

[13]The efficient and formal causes are identified with the motions in the semen at *Gen. An.* 734b28–735a3. For a discussion, see Alan Gotthelf, "Aristotle's Conception of Final Causality," *Review of Metaphysics*, 30 (Dec. 1976), 239–240. I said earlier (Chapter 1, note 10) that Aristotle standardly cites objects rather than events as examples of efficient causes. When he calls the male parent the efficient cause of a generation he is following standard procedure. But, in his discussion of the efficient cause of animal generation in *Generation of Animals*, Aristotle loosens up his terminology; he says that it makes no difference whether we say "the semen" or "that from which the semen comes" (the male parent) when stating the efficient cause. And this is because the efficient cause is whatever is responsible for the motions in the semen, and although they *originate* with the male parent, they also exist *independently* of the male parent, in the semen. Hence, both the male parent and the semen have a legitimate claim to be the efficient cause because in each the motions of the generation originate. But this is not the whole story. The male parent is the efficient cause, the origin of the movement, because he has the appropriate form in actuality; he is actually a human being. The semen is the efficient cause because it contains the motions which express the form of the animal. So, in specifying exactly why and how both the male parent and the semen can be called the efficient cause of the generation, Aristotle makes intrinsic reference to the notion of form. One cannot specify the efficient cause, whether object or event, of animal generation independently of the form.

priate materials and tools. In both cases, of course, the
process can be interrupted and thwarted by adverse circumstances. Nonetheless, in both cases, the power to create is
primarily located by Aristotle in an agent. In the case of
craft production, the agent is the artist by virtue of the art
or definition in the artist's mind. In the case of natural reproduction, the agent is the motions in the semen by virtue
of the form they express.[14]

This discussion raises a number of important issues for consideration. First, the analogy between the artist and form raises
the suspicion that Aristotle thinks of natures (forms) as conscious forces acting intentionally to achieve their ends. And, a
related point, it suggests that Aristotle's emphasis on the role
of form in the workings of nature is a consequence of drawing
a mistaken analogy between art and nature. I shall consider
these points at the end of the next section, after we have considered Aristotle's conception of teleology and his defense of
teleological explanations. Now, however, we shall look at the
two candidates that Aristotle considers to be the chief con-
tenders for being the natures of natural beings: namely, form
and matter. Of course, we know from the foregoing discussion
of generation that Aristotle gives priority to form; but, in order
to understand that verdict, it is important to get clearer on his
conception of the two candidates.

Some people, Aristotle says, think of the nature and substance of natural beings as their matter—"the primary constituent present in it [the natural being]" (193a9–11), "the
primary underlying matter in each case" (193a28–30). He
cites as examples the wood of a bed and the bronze of a
statue. However, it is possible to distinguish two distinct
meanings covered by this use of the term "nature." According to one view, the matter in question is the proximate
matter, or the matter that immediately constitutes the ob-

[14]This remark requires elaboration. What is meant by the form in the context
of embryo development? During embryo development, the form itself is
undergoing a process of actualization; it is neither fully actual nor an individual
at the outset (*Gen. An.* 734b18–19). As more and more organs develop, more
capacities of the form (i.e., soul) are actualized.

ject. The examples of wood and bronze illustrate this position; the nature of a bed is the wood that composes it, and
the object's matter is the origin of those motions which it
undergoes owing to its nature. For convenience, I shall refer to this account of the nature of entities with inner principles of motion and rest as the "materialist account."

Aristotle also considers a second way of taking "nature" to
refer to matter, a view that I call the "reductive materialist
account." On this view, the various sorts of proximate matter
(e.g., the wood and bronze cited above) are seen as reducible
to an underlying matter or matters (193a17–22). For example,
the wood that composes the bed may itself be composed out
of water and earth. According to this view, "matter" refers to
the ultimate, rather than the proximate, matter. Several Greek
philosophers of nature appear to have held to some form of
reductive materialism (e.g., Thales, the Atomists). Aristotle's
primary interest, though, lies in outlining and analyzing the
strategy of a reductive materialist, rather than in considering
any particular example of such a strategy: "Hence fire, earth,
air, and water have been held to be the nature of things, some
people choosing just one for this role, some several, and some
making use of all" (193a22–24). For the reductive materialist,
all other beings and forms of being, such as a bed or, for that
matter, wood, are "merely affections, states, or dispositions"
of the underlying matter (193a25–26).

Both versions of materialism are portrayed by Aristotle as
having held that one could explain the behavior of natural
beings in terms of their matter, either proximate or ultimate.
The notion of matter introduced in this text has some distinctive
features. First, it is identified as a subject, or underlying thing;
second, it is described as an object's inner principle, which is
supposed to be the origin of that object's behavior, i.e., motion
and rest. In the face of this characterization of matter, contemporary philosophers might feel that two distinct issues have
converged: namely, the question of ontological reduction and
the appropriate causal analysis of the behavior of natural
beings. We might think that, whatever the verdict on reduc-
tionism, the appropriate causal analysis of natural beings is to

be given in mechanistic terms and not by appeal to an inner nature, whether that nature be conceived of as form or as matter. It is important to appreciate that Aristotle's notion of matter, unlike ours, is of something that could be the inner origin of a natural being's behavior.

Aristotle is not concerned at this point to do more than simply introduce the concept of nature employed by materialists. Indeed, he mentions only one, rather weak consideration in favor of the view: if you plant a bed, a branch might sprout—but never another bed (193a12–14). As I mentioned above, however, materialist theories had been put forward by several natural philosophers, and Aristotle no doubt felt that their authority legitimated serious consideration of those theories.

There is a second way of conceiving of the nature of a natural being: "It is also used for the shape and form which accords with a thing's account" (193a30–31). If we think of an artifact such as a bed, we can analyze it into two components: (i) the woody matter and (ii) whatever it is about the shape of the wood that causes it to be a bed, rather than a hatrack. In general, the distinction between matter and form is most easily illustrated by artifacts. For we can normally think of a number of things that can be made out of wood—and form is just what accounts for the differences between a wooden bed and a wooden hatrack. We can also think of making an artifact such as a bed out of a number of materials—and form is just what accounts for the similarity between a wooden bed and a brass bed. In the process of making a bed, the artisan changes the matter in such a way that what was a tree is now a bed: the matter is the bed only potentially; after acquiring the form, it is an actual bed. Similarly, Aristotle says: "that which is flesh or bone only potentially, before it acquires the form which accords with the account by which we define what flesh or bone is, does not yet have its proper nature, and is not a thing due to nature" (193a36–b3).

According to the second way of using the term, then, an object's "nature" is identified as its form, which is said to be the definable element in the composite. It is obvious that the second way of thinking of nature (i.e., as form) is inspired by Plato's theory of Forms or Ideas. This heritage is particularly clear in the close relation between definition and form, a central feature of Plato's theory in which forms were introduced primarily as the objects of definitions. Unlike Plato's Forms, which are transcendent objects of definition existing separately from their instances, Aristotle describes his forms as not separable from the composite except in account (193b5–6). No Aristotelian form exists separately from the composite whose form it is, although its definition is not dependent upon the existence of any particular exemplar. I shall discuss the relations between matter, form, and composite in greater detail in Chapter 4.

The claim of form to be identified as the nature of things has to be taken seriously because of its Platonic origin. In addition, Aristotle mentions some brief observations in favor of form. Relying on the analogy with artifacts mentioned above, Aristotle argues that an actual being (i.e., one having form) is called something (e.g., a horse or flower) rather than a potential being. He also notes that natural beings (e.g., human beings) reproduce in kind; if a bed "producing" wood is meant to favor thinking of nature as matter, then a human being producing a human being should count in favor of form. Finally, if we think of how a blob of matter gradually becomes something, and realize that we identify the blob with the end of the process, then it makes more sense to consider the form to be its nature. For example, we think of a human embryo in the uterus as a developing human being and not a developed zygote.

None of the considerations that Aristotle puts forward in favor of either candidate is compelling; indeed, none of them is so intended. Rather, Aristotle is following his dialectical approach to philosophical issues by introducing two respected traditional accounts one could give concerning the natures of natural beings; in each case, he briefly spells out the position and adds some brief remarks on its initial plausibility. To understand Aristotle's argument in favor of the account of nature in terms of the concept of form, we shall have to consider his argument in favor of teleological explanations of natural beings. For the latter also serves as his argument in favor of form.

2. Aristotle's Teleology

In *Physics* ii.1, Aristotle has explained that there are two ways of conceiving of the inner principle of motion and rest possessed by natural beings: one can think of it in terms of the being's matter or in terms of its form. But, for the student of nature, this disjunction is not exclusive. In fact, in chapter 2, Aristotle compares the student of nature with the artisan in regard to their ranges of expertise:

> But if art imitates nature, and it belongs to the same branch of knowledge to know the form and to know the matter up to a point (thus the doctor has knowledge of health, and also of bile and phlegm, the things in which health resides; and the builder knows the form of a house, and also the matter—that it is bricks and beams; and it is the same with other arts), then it belongs to the study of nature to know both sorts of nature. [194a21–28]

A potter must understand both the material used in his or her craft and the craft itself, the principles of design and use that govern the sorts of pottery to be made. Analogously, the student of nature must understand the material side of the organism he or she is studying—how the different sorts of matter act on one another, for example, as well as its form.

One way to understand Aristotle's position is to imagine two levels of facts to be explained about a given organism, an animal.[15] Some of the facts about the animal (e.g., its eye color

---

[15]My understanding of Aristotle's argument for teleology is much indebted to John Cooper (although my interpretation diverges from his at some points). See Cooper, "Aristotle on Natural Teleology," in *Language and Logos: Studies in Ancient Greek Philosophy*, ed. Malcolm Schofield and Martha Craven Nussbaum (Cambridge: Cambridge University Press, 1982), pp. 197–222.

My interpretation differs from Cooper's as follows. First of all, in his explanation of the generation of an animal, Cooper divides Aristotle's causes into (i) material and efficient and (ii) formal and final. For Cooper, form is an

or female sex) are caused by its matter and, hence, are to be explained by reference to matter alone.[16] Other facts (e.g., that it is a cow) are caused by form, and hence are to be explained by reference to form. When a blue-eyed cow is generated, the matter involved is the inner origin of the process that results in the color of its eyes; whereas the form is the inner origin of the process that results in those organs which cows have, including incidentally the eyes—i.e., the process of cow development.

It is important to notice that, according to this picture, both the natural being's form and its matter can operate as an inner origin of motion, i.e., as an efficient cause. For this reason, it is a mistake to group the matter and the efficient cause together and to distinguish them from the formal and final causes.[17] Rather, natural beings have an inner principle or origin of motion and rest; in relation to some motions the principle is to be identified with its form, and in relation to others it is to be identified with its matter. With regard to natural causation,

---

efficient cause only in the sense that the male parent is an efficient cause (pp. 201–202). On my view, Aristotle thinks of the form of the developing offspring as the efficient cause of the process (see note 13, above, and note 17 below). Second, Cooper holds that the key to understanding Aristotle's teleology is Aristotle's belief that the species are eternal. Although I tend to think that Aristotle did hold that the species are eternal, I do not see that belief as playing a central role in his justification of teleology.

[16]Aristotle assigns responsibility to the matter when a *female* offspring is the result of the generation. For a discussion of the roles of matter and form in relation to different attributes of the offspring, see my paper "Form, Reproduction, and Inherited Characteristics in Aristotle's *Generation of Animals*," *Phronesis*, 30 (1985), 46–57.

[17]Although I think that the contrast between material/efficient causation and formal/final causation is a misrepresentation of Aristotle's discussion of matter, form, and natural beings in *Physics* II, Aristotle does on occasion discuss the topic of causes in terms that might suggest such an opposition. For example, criticizing earlier philosophers, he says that some grasped only the material cause, others the material and efficient causes (*Metaph.* 1. 4. 985a10–14). Plato, on the other hand, is described as using formal and material causes and, presumably, ignoring the efficient cause (988a7–10). Aristotle uses his own four causes in these contexts as a framework for pointing out what is lacking or unclear in his predecessors' views. The fact that Aristotle describes some of them as using material/efficient causation does not establish that *Aristotle* thought that only matter could be an origin or principle of motion (i.e., an efficient cause).

then, Aristotle does not envision two levels—a materialistic-mechanistic level contrasted with and supplemented by a formal-teleological one—but, rather, two kinds of efficient causes or origins of motion: namely, matter and form. Some processes originate in, or are originated by, the organism's matter; others are originated by its form.

So far in our story, matter and form have been treated in an egalitarian fashion. But Aristotle does not, ultimately, endorse this sort of egalitarian vision of the natural world: "The student of nature should state both causes, but particularly the cause which is what the thing is for; for that is responsible for the matter, whilst the matter is not responsible for the end" (200a32–34).[18] We are now in a position to ask two questions. First, why does Aristotle think that some phenomena involving natural beings are caused by formal or final causes, rather than by material causes? Second, why does he assign priority to formal and final causes over material causes in his explanation of the behavior of natural beings?

I have begun referring to formal *and* final causes; so, before addressing the first of my two questions, it is necessary to introduce the notion of a final cause, and to explain its connection with form or formal cause. In his discussion of the range of study of the student of nature, Aristotle says: "Further, it belongs to the same study to know the end or what something is for, and to know whatever is for that end. Now nature is an end and what something is for" (*Physics* II.2.194a27–29; also *Parts An.* I.641b24–27). In *Physics* II.3, in his enumeration of the four causes, Aristotle lists matter, form, the efficient cause, and the final cause—"And again, a thing may be a cause as the end. That is what something is for, as health may be what a walk is for " (194b33–34).

Later, Aristotle says that the student of nature should know all four causes and use all of them in response to the question "Why?" (II.7.198a17–22). Does Aristotle think that there are *three* ways to use the term "nature" in connection with natural

[18]The greater importance of the final cause is also stressed in *Parts of Animals* I.1.642a13–30.

beings—form, matter, and end? He does not. For he holds that, in the case of natural beings, the formal and final causes coincide:

> What a thing is, and what it is for, are one and the same, and that from which the change originates is the same in form as these. Thus a man gives birth to a man, and so it is in general with things which are themselves changed in changing other things—and things which are not so changed fall beyond the study of nature. [198a25–27][19]

We know that, for Aristotle, a natural being's form is correlated with the definition of that being. We know that a final cause, or end, is what a thing or process is for; it is a goal. How are we to understand the identification of these two distinct concepts in the case of natural beings? Let us consider a process that we used in distinguishing natural and nonnatural beings: namely, the process of generation. The final cause or goal of this process is the formation of an animal like in kind to its parents.[20] The final cause or goal of reproduction is a being of a certain type, one that exhibits the appropriate form. The goal of the generation is to achieve its form.[21]

Aristotle's teleology is not restricted to explanation of the generation of natural beings; in his biological writings, it also permeates his explanation of their organs and behavior. One can and should explain what an organ is in terms of the function it has to perform (*Parts An.* 645b14–21). For example, a bodily organ such as the eye ought to be explained functionally, in

---

[19]Aristotle also identifies final and formal causes at *Physics* 199a31–33 and *Parts of Animals* 639b14–21.

[20]In the paper cited in note 16 above, I argue that the form of the offspring does not include its inherited characteristics (e.g., eye color). The goal or end of the generation is an animal of the same kind, not a replication of the male parent.

[21]This explanation of the connection between formal and final cause might seem to undermine my earlier claim that the form is the inner origin of the process of generation. How can form be at work on the matter *and* be the goal or end of the generation? In note 14 above, I explained that the form is becoming actualized during the process of generation. The end, or final cause, is the actualization of the form in appropriate matter; and that is just the creation of a new substance.

terms of an activity that is its end; eyes exist for the sake of sight, and that is the central element in their definition. Activities of living beings are also to be understood teleologically, in terms of how they contribute to other activities that are central to a being of that kind. The stalking behavior of a carnivore, for example, should be be understood teleologically; such behavior is for the sake of nutrition, which is a core (definitional) activity of animals.

In addition, there is an evaluative aspect to Aristotle's teleology. For he frequently describes the goal or end of a change in value language, i.e., as for the good or because it is better. For example, in *Metaphysics* I, Aristotle criticizes his materialist predecessors for not explaining the goodness and beauty inherent in natural changes:

> When these men and the principles of this kind had had their day, as the latter were found inadequate to generate the nature of things, men were again forced by the truth itself, as we said, to inquire into the next kind of cause. For it is not likely either that fire or earth or any such element should be the reason why things manifest goodness and beauty both in their being and in their coming to be, or that those thinkers should have supposed it was; nor again could it be right to entrust so great a matter to spontaneity and chance. [984b8–14; also see 983a31–32, 988b6–16]

What does Aristotle think needs explanation? In what way do plants and animals exhibit goodness and beauty? Let us consider the example of the generation of an animal. The idea is that the form, or the design, of an animal is good in the sense of "good for that animal"; so the process toward the actualization of that form or design is a process toward a good. The design is good for the animal in the sense that it is best, or at least well suited, for the range of activities that the animal engages in (those activities being constitutive of the essence of an animal of that kind).

In a rather extensive discussion of the views of other philosophers, Aristotle tells us that they all—with the notable exception of Plato—tried to explain the behavior and formation of natural beings solely in terms of material and efficient causes, making no mention of formal or final causes.[22] With their views in mind, Aristotle opens *Physics* II.8 with this statement:

> We must first give reasons for including nature among causes which are for something, and then turn to the necessary, and see how it is present in that which is natural. For everyone brings things back to this cause, saying that because the hot is by nature such as to be thus, and similarly the cold and everything else of that sort, therefore these things come to be and are. [198b10–14]

Aristotle has two projects in chapters 8 and 9. The first is to argue for viewing the life processes, structure, and behavior of natural beings as teleological, as caused by ends; the second is to consider how material necessity operates in the natural realm. Once Aristotle has established that the behavior of natural beings must be explained by means of final causes, he considers how the principles used by his physicist predecessors (i.e., the necessary causal interactions of matter) fit into the teleological story. In examining Aristotle's arguments in these two chapters, we will be addressing the questions with which we began: (i) Why does Aristotle think that the behavior of natural beings requires an understanding of final as well as material causes? (ii) Why does he also think that final causes are more important?

Before turning to Aristotle's argument, it is important to underline two features of my interpretation that may not be immediately apparent. On my interpretation, Aristotle holds that the form or end of natural beings is responsible for a significant portion of their behavior; hence, the natural philosopher ought to explain that behavior in terms of formal or final causation. What this means is that the behavior in question cannot be given an adequate explanation in purely material-efficient terms; explanations in terms of material and formal

---

[22]Aristotle discusses his predecessors' views on causation at some length in *Metaphysics* I, chapters 3–10.

causation are not two alternative options, each adequate to a different pragmatic context of explanation or description of the event or behavior to be explained.[23] Rather, explanation in terms of material and efficient causation alone is, Aristotle argues in the *Physics*, inadequate for the behavior of natural beings because there can be no causal account of that behavior in those terms alone.[24]

The second point concerns the ontological status of forms and ends. Aristotle thinks that forms and ends really exist in nature. Explanation in terms of material and efficient causation is inadequate because there is another cause responsible for the behavior of natural beings. Aristotle's point is not that an appeal to ends makes explanation of the behavior of natural beings simpler or more intelligible, for that position is fully compatible with the view that a complete account can be given in material-efficient terms.[25] For example, one could hold that

[23]Scholarly opinion is divided on the issue of how to understand the formal cause. Waterlow and Cooper, in the works cited (notes 4 and 15 above), think Aristotle assigns the concept real causal efficacy. The notion that the four causes are four "becauses," or explanations, is discussed in Richard Sorabji, *Necessity, Cause, and Blame* (Ithaca: Cornell University Press, 1980), pp. 40–42. Bas van Fraassen connects the four kinds of explanation to pragmatic contexts ("The Pragmatics of Explanation," *American Philosophical Quarterly*, 14 [1977], 143–50). Charlton's discussion of the contrast between material and final causation, in terms of the distinction between causes and reasons, suggests that these explanations are appropriate to different descriptions of a particular event or change, i.e., whether or not it is described in intentional terms (*Aristotle's Physics*, pp. 117–118).

[24]The idea that in *Physics* ii.8–9 Aristotle rules out the possibility of a causally sufficient account of natural phenomena in purely material terms has been challenged recently by David Charles. In *Aristotle's Philosophy of Action* (Ithaca: Cornell University Press, 1984), Charles argues that Aristotle both holds actions to be materially necessitated and assigns an explanatory role to forms and ends. In a recent, unpublished paper, "Aristotle on Hypothetical Necessity and Irreducibility," Charles broadens his view to include biological phenomena. In brief, he holds that Aristotle did not rule out the possibility of providing sufficient material conditions for biological processes; indeed, he claims that this is precisely what Aristotle is trying to do in *Generation of Animals, Meteorology*, and other works. I comment on Charles's specific claims in notes 28, 31, and 32 below.

[25]J. L. Mackie describes the compatibility of teleology and efficient causation as follows: "though we have found several uses for distinctively teleological accounts and explanations, we have found no objective processes which are

it is helpful to understand the configuration of a dog's teeth in terms of the functions or ends they serve, without in any way implying that the configuration could not be explained solely in terms of material-efficient causation. Aristotle, in contrast, thinks it is helpful to understand the configuration of the dog's teeth in terms of an end because (i) there are ends operating in nature and (ii) the formation of the dog's teeth is a natural process. It could not be explained in terms of material-efficient causation alone, because that cause is not the only, or indeed the most important, one responsible for the configuration.

Why think that there are ends in nature that are causally responsible for the behavior of natural beings? Consider, Aristotle says, the phenomenon of rainfall and its relation to another periodic occurrence, the growth of corn. Rain falls as a consequence of a series of events, all caused by a sequence of material-efficient factors: water evaporates, cools, and then falls as rain. The fact that rainfall results in the growth of corn is merely a coincidence, not its end or goal (*Physics* 198b17–20). Could we not explain the configuration of an animal's teeth in a similar manner? Could it not be a fully necessitated material process, whose outcome happens to be beneficial for the animal (198b24–29)? These examples highlight two components in the rival, materialist explanation of the formation of the parts of natural beings that we have not yet discussed: namely, that the processes occur by necessity and by coincidence. In order to understand the view that Aristotle will argue against, and in order to understand the terms of his argument, we need to understand these two features of the rival, materialist account.

First of all, let us consider the notion that Aristotle's materialist opponents held that natural processes occur according to necessity. Aristotle describes the materialist as explaining phenomena in terms of the mechanistic interactions of matter,

---

in themselves teleological in a way which precludes their being instances of efficient causation" (*The Cement of the Universe* [Oxford: Oxford University Press, 1974], p. 295).

in which the behavior and outcome of the interaction are solely a function of the conditions and the various matters present. Moreover, the outcomes are necessary. The matters used in causal explanations have their own natures, and it is through the combination and interactions of these material natures that all change is explained:

> Now those who in ancient times were the first to philosophize about nature were thinking about the material origin and sort of cause—what and what kind of thing is matter, how does the universe come to be out of it, and with what cause of movement (such as strife or love or mind or spontaneity), assuming that the underlying matter has a certain kind of nature by necessity—fire a hot nature and earth a cold one, the former light and the latter heavy. For this is how they generate the universe. [*Parts An.* 1.1.640b5–12]

The necessity in question attaches to the processes of interaction among material components, given that each has the nature that it has. The outcome, for example, of combining a certain portion of fire (which is hot) and of earth (which is cold) is necessary from the outset, given the natures in question and the amounts of each. In this paragraph, Aristotle has been describing a reductive materialist account of causation—an account that envisions an explanation from basic stuffs to the whole universe—and it is appropriate to point out here that, so far as we can tell, in Aristotle's time there were no detailed scientific or philosophical proposals to bridge this immense gap. Perhaps it is for this reason that Aristotle, in his argument in the *Physics*, does not directly address the reductive materialist proposal.[26] Instead, he describes the issue as a contrast between an explanation in terms of proximate, material-efficient causation and an explantion in terms of final and formal causation.

What is now puzzling is why Aristotle describes this sort of

[26]From the contemporary perspective, of course, the reductive materialist position is the strongest alternative position to Aristotle's. From Aristotle's perspective, however, the reductive materialism of the Atomists was less compelling than the kind of materialism he attributes to Empedocles.

materialist explanation of change as not only by necessity but also as coincidental. To modern ears, the description "by necessity" seems to exclude the description "by coincidence."[27] For if the interaction between fire and earth occurs by necessity (i.e., the outcome is necessitated given the amounts of each and their natures), then how can this picture of causation be described as also coincidental, which implies that the outcome is random? The answer is to be found in a careful consideration of what Aristotle means by a "coincidence."

Imagine, to begin with, the following story. A person goes to the market to buy tomatoes and, instead of buying tomatoes, bumps into a friend who repays an outstanding loan. This sequence is an example of a coincidence; because it is in the realm of human action, Aristotle says it occurs "by luck." The crucial feature is that the event, the collecting of the debt, could have been the goal of an action undertaken to achieve it, but it was not. In Aristotle's terms, it might have come to be for something or for an end (*Physics* 197a32–35). The person might have gone to the market to find her friend to collect the debt, but she did not do so; the outcome was not the goal of her action (which was to purchase tomatoes) but, rather, an accidental outcome.

Aristotle calls coincidences in the realm of nature "the automatic," a broader term including events that occur by luck. Lucky events are distinguished from the automatic ones because, in the former events, the agent chooses and is capable of choosing the end in question. Coincidences in the realm of nature are also such that they might happen for an end, but it is not an end chosen by an agent: "Plainly, then, in the field of things which in a general way come to be for something, if something comes to be but not for that which supervenes, and has an external cause, we say that it is an automatic outcome; and if such an outcome is for something capable of choosing and is an object of

---

[27]Waterlow offers an excellent discussion of the relationship between the notions "by necessity" and "by coincidence" (*Nature, Change, and Agency*, p. 75).

object of choice, we call it the outcome of luck" (197b18–22). Let us consider Aristotle's notion of the coincidental in nature in connection with the example of rain and corn. The falling of rain, according to this example, is fully necessitated by material factors. On the other hand, it is good for the corn; indeed, watering corn is the sort of event that can occur for an end—Zeus could send rain for that purpose. What is coincidental is not the rain falling, but its beneficial effect on the corn. It is coincidental because the rain did not fall in order to accomplish that end; the end simply happened to happen. Nonetheless, the rainfall itself was fully necessitated by material factors. In calling the connection between rain falling and corn flourishing coincidental, Aristotle is denying neither that the rainfall was necessary nor that corn flourishes when it is watered (and a materialist account can be envisioned for this occurrence). Rather, the conjunction of the two events is coincidental because neither happened for the sake of the other. An event is coincidental when it does not happen for the sake of the end that results; the coincidental is contrasted with the teleological, not with the necessary.

The development of the various parts of animals can be explained in a fashion similar to the proposed explanation of rainfall. Consider the development of an animal's teeth: "What, then, is to stop parts in nature, too, from being like this—the front teeth of necessity growing sharp and suitable for biting, and the back teeth broad and serviceable for chewing the food, not coming to be *for* this, but by coincidence? And similarly with the other parts in which the 'for something' seems to be present" (198b24–27). The development of teeth is a good example of an occurrence that appears to occur for an end; the functional value of having teeth is rather obvious. But, Aristotle says, is it not possible that in this case, and in other like cases, the teeth really do not come to be for the sake of the good of the animal in question, but, rather, are formed by purely efficient-material causes working necessarily? That the end product, the teeth of various sorts in a useful configuration, is good for the animal is purely coincidental. According to this account of the development of natural beings, the fact that we by and large observe well-adapted parts of animals is because those animals with useless or badly adapted parts did not survive. What we see around us is the result of pure coincidence. Organisms with poor constitutions simply did not last long: "So when all turned out just as if they had come to be for something, then the things, suitably constituted as an automatic outcome, survived; when not, they died, and die, as Empedocles says of the man-headed calves" (198b29–32).

The account that Aristotle will argue against makes three basic claims:

> (1) Natural phenomena, such as the formation of animal parts, can be fully explained in terms of material-efficient causation.

> (2) That the products are useful for the animal, or that they function well, is purely a matter of coincidence. The processes are such that they might have occurred for that end, but as a matter of fact they do not.

> (3) The explanation for the fact that we see many examples of this sort of coincidence around us (e.g., useful organs) is that those animals with organs that happen not to contribute to their good do not survive, whereas those animals with organs that do happen to contribute to their good flourish.

Aristotle offers the following argument (198b33–a8) to establish that the rival account is impossible:

> (1) All things that are owing to nature (including such processes as the formation of teeth in animals) come to be as they do always or for the most part.

> (2) Nothing that is the outcome of luck or the automatic, i.e., coincidental, comes to be always or for the most part.

> (3) Things happen either coincidentally or for the sake of something.

> (4) Therefore, the sorts of phenomena in question occur for something.

(5) And since all parties to the dispute say that the phenomena under discussion are owing to nature,

(6) The "for something" or end is present in things that are and that come to be owing to nature.

The conclusion of the argument is that formal and final causes operate in those things which are owing to nature. And this conclusion means that material necessitation alone is not causally sufficient for natural processes.[28] The argument does not establish, and is not intended to establish, that material necessities are not operative in nature. Rather, Aristotle argues that another causal factor is at work.

The argument is generally conceded to be valid, and most critical evaluations have centered on the truth of the premises. In my discussion, I restrict my criticisms to those points which it is reasonable to think might have been voiced by his opponent. Contemporary philosophers might be inclined to raise a number of issues that would not have troubled Aristotle's interlocutors. For example, we might be inclined to question Aristotle's premise (3) on the grounds that the alternatives

---

[28]I understand the conclusion of Aristotle's argument to rule out *in principle* the possibility of a causally sufficient, purely material account of natural processes. David Charles has argued (private correspondence) that the conclusion should be read more narrowly, as a criticism of the adequacy of Empedocles' materialist account, and Charles mentions as a parallel Aristotle's criticisms (in *Gen. An.*) of the details of Empedocles' account of animal generation. Why not treat Aristotle's argument (in the *Physics*) against Empedocles' version of materialism as a criticism of the specific details of the account, rather than as against materialist accounts generally? The answer is that in the *Physics*, in contrast to *Generation of Animals*, Aristotle does not criticize the details of Empedocles' view. Rather, he uses Empedocles' account as an example of a theory that uses material necessity and coincidence to explain natural generation, and he tries to argue that any account that uses just these two categories is inadequate. The argument answers the question posed earlier: How should we think of nature? And the materialist alternative is not identified with the views of Empedocles. Since Aristotle concludes this argument with the claim that goals or ends are required to account for natural generation, it is far more plausible, given the context, to interpret Aristotle as thinking that he has ruled out materialist accounts generally. After all, if Aristotle thought that he had ruled out only one particular materialist account, why would he feel entitled to the conclusion that ends or goals are required to account for natural processes?

presented are not exhaustive. We might be inclined to object that natural phenomena occur neither coincidentally nor for an end, but in accordance with the laws of nature. The laws of nature operate regularly, and so natural phenomena are not coincidences; but the laws of nature are not teleological, and so natural phenomena do not occur for an end. It should be remembered, however, that Aristotle is treating his view and his opponent's view as the two going alternatives, and there is no reason to think his opponents would object to premise (3). But it is not clear that Aristotle's materialist opponent would have any reason to accept the first two premises. In what follows, I suggest two readings of the first two premises. In each case, Aristotle's opponent would have reason to reject one of the premises, and so I conclude that this argument, as it stands, is insufficient to decide the issue between Aristotle and his materialist opponent.

The first alternative reads the phrase "always or for the most part" in a *strong sense* in premises (1) and (2). According to this reading, Aristotle is claiming in the first premise that natural processes occur *eternally* in a fixed pattern; in the second premise he is saying that no coincidental occurrence is *eternal.*[29] Although this reading renders premise (2) acceptable to Aristotle's opponent, it seems unlikely that premise (1) would be accepted on this understanding. For, as Aristotle has just told us, Empedocles does *not* believe in eternally fixed species; indeed, his view holds that many unsuccessful organisms have died off in the past. The fact that Aristotle has just described this feature of his opponent's view counts against this reading, for Aristotle does not offer any argument or reason for his opponent to change his mind.

The other reading takes "always or for the most part" in both premises in a *weaker sense*, as simply referring to what can be observed in ordinary experience, observations that would have been enriched and multiplied by Aristotle's systematic observation of nature. Premise (1) records Aristotle's wide experi-

---

[29]This is the interpretation argued for in Cooper, "Aristotle on Natural Teleology."

ence of the regularity of natural processes, a regularity that he thinks his opponent would also have to acknowledge. Aristotle has good reason to assert this premise, for in biological research he had seen a lot of evidence of how various features of a wide range of organisms were formed in a uniform manner and did contribute to the well-being of those organisms. With this interpretation of (1), however, we must now reconsider premise (2). For surely it is consistent for Aristotle's opponent to explain the widespread uniformity of nature as the product of a series of favorable coincidences and the elimination of unsuccessful arrangements. We see around us beneficial arrangements of animal parts because, over a long period of time, animals with detrimental arrangements died out, leaving only well-formed animals to reproduce.

This explanation sounds more appealing to our modern ears than it would have to Aristotle and his contemporaries. To them, it would have been pure hypothesis; the world around them contained no evidence of the earlier existence of ill-adapted beings. There would be no evidence to count in favor of Empedocles' story. Still, it remains a possibility that counts against premise (2), and so I conclude that Aristotle's argument does not establish that final causes are operative in nature. On the other hand, Aristotle's rejection of Empedocles' story, given the evidence then available, was reasonable. And so it is easy to appreciate why Aristotle might have thought that the argument did indeed establish the need for final causality.[30]

At this stage of the argument, Aristotle has established that final causes are operative in the realm of nature. Final causes, or ends, are responsible for both the generation of natural beings (animals, plants) and the structure and functioning of their organic parts. The materialists were wrong in thinking that material necessity alone is responsible for natural processes and structures. What is not yet determined is (i) the extent of the causal responsibility of Aristotelian forms or ends

---

[30]In the rest of chapter 8, Aristotle supplements his argument by listing a number of points in favor of the proposal that there are ends operative in nature. The list is a jumble of different sorts of considerations, none of them particularly convincing.

and (ii) to what extent Aristotle accommodates the materialist point of view. At first glance, Aristotle's position might appear to be a compromise between the materialist view and Platonic formalism. For Aristotle holds that the student of nature must understand both material nature and formal nature. The compromise is only apparent, however, for in chapter 9 of the *Physics* Aristotle argues that the formal and final causes are more important than the material cause (thereby demoting the materialist's preferred mode of explanation from equal partner to junior partner). And, as part of the demotion of matter and material causes, Aristotle argues that material necessity is not simple necessity (as the materialists thought) but, rather, hypothetical necessity. The necessity that Aristotle attributes to matter is hypothetical; it is necessity in relation to some goal or end. Not only are material necessities less important than forms or ends in the correct causal analysis of natural phenomena, but material necessities, correctly understood, do not operate independently of goals or ends. These two points constitute Aristotle's asymmetrical distribution of causal responsibility to matter and form in relation to natural phenomena.

In what follows, I discuss each point in turn, beginning with the issue of material necessity. To illustrate the materialist account of material necessity, Aristotle discusses an example of an artifact:

> The general view is that things come to be of necessity, in the way in which a man might think that a city wall came to be of necessity, if he thought that since heavy things are by nature such as to sink down, and light to rise to the surface, the stones and foundations go down, the earth goes above them because it is lighter, and the posts go on top because they are lightest of all. Now without these things no city wall would have come to be; still it was not on account of them, except as matter, that it came to be, but for the protection and preservation of certain things. [199b35–200a7]

Aristotle's point is that material nature has a role to play in the generation of things; foundations are made out of heavy matter. But that material nature is utilized to build a wall *only if* another causal factor is present—the final cause. Similarly, in the generation of an animal, certain materials are needed, and they interact with one another according to their natures. The sperm from the male parent, for example, is hot and is described by Aristotle as setting, or curdling, the cooler matter from the female. But to suppose that this material necessity— that so much hot matter will have a certain effect on a certain amount of another sort of matter—is the cause of the generation of an animal is just like supposing that the relative weights and positions of boards and stones is the cause of the production of a wall.

Our response to these examples is twofold. We might agree with Aristotle that if this is what the materialist means by material necessity, then something crucial has been left out of the causal story. On the other hand, we might disagree with Aristotle over *what* has been left out of the story. Aristotle says that what has been left out is the goal or end of the process ("the protection and preservation of certain things"). We might think that what is needed to supplement the material cause is the efficient cause, or causes, not the formal or final cause. What is needed to explain the building of a wall or the generation of an animal, in addition to a list of ingredients, is an account of the sequence of efficient causes that constitute those processes. Of course, it is inadequate to explain the building of a wall solely in terms of the material natures of its constituents: someone places the stones and foundations on the bottom. And, in the case of the generation of an animal, we need to understand what brings the sperm in proximity with the matter, and what causes the "curdling" process to occur. Why does Aristotle say that what is missing in the account is the final cause, rather than point to what is obviously missing: namely, the efficient cause?

At this juncture, it is helpful to recall that Aristotle considers both form and matter as candidates for being efficient causes. More concretely, Aristotle thinks that an artisan is an efficient cause by virtue of the art (definition) he or she has in mind, and Aristotle thinks that the form is the efficient cause of the

generation of an animal. It is the definition or art of wallbuild-
ing in the artisan's mind that causes the motions that place the
stones on the bottom (the form or art is the goal or end that
the artisan is trying to achieve). In the case of animal generation, it is the form conveyed by motions in the semen that
guides the material interactions so that they constitute a process
of embryonic development (the realization of its form is the
goal or end that it is trying to achieve).[31]

My explanation of Aristotle's position might appear to contain a conceptual contradiction concerning the notion of a
cause; for it says that the efficient cause of the wall, or of the
animal, is its form or end. If we think of Aristotelian efficient
causes as events that precede their effects, this interpretation
might appear contradictory. For if we were to think of efficient
causes in this way, then it would be difficult to see how either
matter or form could count as an efficient cause, since neither
matter nor form is an event. So, it is very important at this
juncture to recall what I said about Aristotelian causes in Chapter 1 (§ 2) There I pointed out that Aristotle's causes (including
the efficient cause) are objects, rather than events; and I cau-
tioned against understanding his causes (even his efficient
cause) to be events, as we do today. Once we understand that
Aristotle's efficient causes are objects and not events, then his
position that form, rather than matter, is the efficient cause
of the housebuilding or the animal becomes conceptually
coherent.

Where do material natures and material necessity fit into this
causal picture? Once Aristotle has assigned primary (efficient)
causal responsibility to forms and ends, the role of matter and
material necessities must be reconsidered. Aristotle's view is
that the presence of certain kinds and amounts of matter are

---

[31]David Charles (*Aristotle's Philosophy of Action*) holds that, far from ruling
out the possibility of a causally sufficient account of animal reproduction in
purely material terms, Aristotle is developing just such an account in *Generation
of Animals*. It is hard to see how Charles could make a convincing argument
for this claim in light of the fact that Aristotle identifies the origin of motion
(efficient cause) of the process of generation with what is contained in the
semen, which is the form or soul (*Gen. An.* 734b23–25).

a necessary, but never a sufficient, condition of a production or a generation: "Now without these things [building materials] no city wall would have come to be; still it was not on account of them, except as matter, that it came to be, but for the protection and preservation of certain things." One needs a certain quantity of rigid materials to build a wall; if one is to build a wall, then there must be certain materials present. The necessity here is hypothetical. But no unconditional necessity attaches to the matter: the presence of certain materials in certain quantities does not necessitate a wall. The materialists were wrong in thinking of material necessity as they did. Material necessity in relation both to artificial and natural processes is hypothetical—certain matter is necessary in order to realize a certain goal or structure or behavior.

Earlier in this section I suggested that a useful way to begin to understand Aristotle's position concerning nature as matter and nature as form is to think about two levels or kinds of facts to be explained about an organism. Some such facts are caused by an organism's form, and some are caused by its matter; our example of the former was the formation of a cow's eye, our example of the latter was eye color. Given what has just been said, this picture requires reconsideration. For if all material necessity is hypothetical necessity, it seems that no facts about the organism can be explained in material terms alone. In fact, Aristotle does seem to think that some features of an organism (its eye color and female sex) and some stages in organic development (the development of *homoeomeroi* such as blood and flesh) can be explained in terms of purely material interaction.[32]

---

[32]Aristotle attributes eye color and female sex to a purely material cause in *Generation of Animals*. And in *Meteorology* IV.12 he says that the formation of *homoeomeroi* (homogeneous biological stuff such as bone, flesh, and sinews) can be explained in terms of purely material interactions (390b2–14). Do these texts exemplify Aristotle's attempts to formulate a materialist account of natural processes, as David Charles claims (note 24 above)? I have already criticized the idea that *Generation of Animals* contains an Aristotelian attempt to provide a causally sufficient account of animal reproduction in terms of material interactions alone (see note 31). Not only does the *Meteorology* not provide such an account, it appears to rule it out. For Aristotle explicitly denies that the formation of bodily parts, whether eyes or hearts, can be explained in purely material terms, i.e., in terms of the material processes he describes at some

But even though Aristotle seems to think that the development of a given eye color or the production of flesh is necessitated by material interactions, these are not processes that occur entirely independently of form. For the sequence of development of an eye is governed by form, and there would be no eye color without an eye. In addition, *homoeomeroi*, stuff such as flesh and bone, exist as parts of organs such as hands and feet; and form governs the sequence of development of hands and feet. Even these material necessities do not operate entirely independently of forms or ends.

From this account of how material necessities fit into Aristotle's teleological account of natural processes, it is quite clear that final causes are far and away the most important causal factors operating in nature. Aristotle expresses the relative importance of material and final causes, the terms in which nature should be explained, as follows: "Plainly, then, the necessary in things which are natural is that which is given as the matter, and the changes it undergoes. The student of nature should state both causes, but particularly the cause which is what the thing is for; for that is the cause of the matter, whilst the matter is not the cause of the end" (200a31–34; also *Parts An.* 641a29–33). The final cause is the cause of the matter, in the sense that it is the goal or end in question that is responsible for the kinds and quantities of matter that must be present. Since a house is a shelter for humans (definition, goal), then it must be built from a certain quantity of certain kinds of materials (bricks, stone, boards). But the matter, its nature and quantity, is not similarly responsible for a certain goal being necessitated. The existence of a certain quantity of bricks or boards does not necessitate the existence of a house. According to Aristotle,

---

length in this treatise. Since Aristotle explicitly denies that bodily parts are formed by material processes alone, the most that this text establishes is that he is willing to explain certain low-level processes of development in material terms alone. Even these processes, however, do not occur entirely independently of form, for these biological stuffs are formed as the materials that constitute organic parts: flesh is the matter of a hand. Since the formation of a hand cannot be given a causally sufficient explanation in material terms alone, and since flesh is only flesh when it is part of a hand, form is indirectly, though not directly, a factor in the formation of flesh.

then, the form or end has dual causal responsibility. It is responsible for the outcome—that there exists a wall or an animal—and it is responsible for the fact that certain materials are necessary or required in order to produce a wall or an animal.

This description of the way in which forms or ends are responsible for the matter raises an issue that I mentioned earlier in this section but postponed for later discussion. The issue concerns to what extent Aristotle conceived of natural ends as conscious forces, and to what extent Aristotle's idea that there are ends operating in nature is a result of a mistaken analogy between art and nature. For Aristotle's position that the goal or end necessitates the matter makes some sense when what you are talking about is artificial production. What is needed to produce a wall or a house is determined by the idea or plan the artisan has in mind. There is a very straightforward and unobjectionable sense in which the goal or plan or art is the cause of certain matter being required. But these sorts of goals or plans exist in minds, and their material implementation requires thought.

Now, let us consider nature and natural phenomena. Here, too, Aristotle thinks that goals or ends are responsible for the matter and responsible for the process as a whole. Does Aristotle conceive of natural goals or ends as conscious agents "selecting" the appropriate matter for their realization? Is his analysis of natural processes the result of a simple error, a mistaken analogy between art and nature?

As to the first point, Aristotle twice states in *Physics* ii. 8, the chapter in which he argues extensively for final causes in nature, that natural ends should not be thought of as involving deliberation, the planning of a conscious agent (199a20–24, 199b27–32). But, this is the basic point of disanalogy between artificial and natural processes that we would have expected Aristotle to have missed if he had been basing his natural teleology on an analogy between art and nature. Further, as we have seen, Aristotle's main argument for final causes in nature makes no appeal to the realm of art. So, even though Aristotle frequently compares the realms of art and nature in his explanation of natural teleology, his central argument for teleology is not based on the analogy. Indeed, he takes some pains to explain that natural goals, unlike goals in art, do not require the deliberation of a conscious agent for their implementation.

Individual, sensible substances are one kind of natural being, and I considered Aristotle's discussion of the hylomorphic constitution of natural beings in order to explain the terms Aristotle uses (*Metaph.* vii–ix) in his discussion of sensible substances. I discussed at some length Aristotle's defense of teleological causal explanations in nature because I believe that his hylomorphic analysis of sensible substances is based upon his teleology. That is to say, as I understand the structure of Aristotle's thought, his argument in favor of the analysis of individual, sensible substances into matter *and* form receives its most extensive defense in his arguments for teleological explanations. It was for this reason that we looked closely at Aristotle's arguments for teleology. This means (although, for concision, I shall not develop the point here) that, on my view, Aristotelian forms and essences are inherently teleological; they are inherently part of a teleological worldview. By "inherently teleological" I mean two things: (i) that Aristotle's argument for teleology constitutes his principal argument for forms or essences, and (ii) that his identification of formal and final causes in the case of natural beings gives their forms, or essences, a teleological dimension. The second point will be fleshed out a bit further in the next chapter (§ 5). I begin the next chapter, which concerns the notion of essence, by drawing together two features of Aristotle's thought on substance: (i) the position discussed in Chapter 2, that substances are prior to, and the principles of, nonsubstances; and (ii) the position discussed in this chapter, that individual, sensible substances are composites of form and matter.

Chapter 4

THE NATURE AND FUNCTION OF ESSENCE

The essence is one of several candidates for being the principle or cause of sensible substance; those candidates are investigated by Aristotle in *Metaphysics* VII–IX.[1] Essence, as I said in Chapter 1 (§ 5), is one of four possible responses to the definitional question—"What is substance?" The definitional question is, for Aristotle, a question concerning principles and causes. So, that question—asked in relation to sensible substances—is a question concerning the principles and causes of sensible substances; and essence is put forward as a possible candidate for that role. In this chapter, I explain that Aristotle does, indeed, hold essence (which he identifies with form) to be the principle or cause of being of composite substances. The assignment of the function "cause of being" to essences raises a number of questions. Why is there a question concerning the cause of being of composite substances? What does it mean to say that essence is the cause of being of composite substances? And what picture of Aristotelian essences emerges from this characterization of their function? This chapter will be concerned to answer these three basic questions about Aristotle's essences. First, however, let us draw together two lines of

[1]See *Metaphysics* VII.3.1028b33–36, VIII.1.1042a12–18.

thought concerning individual, material substances. Doing so will help provide a context for what Aristotle says about their essences.[2]

Imagine that you have analyzed living natural beings into two constituents, matter and form. The matter is, roughly speaking, the body; the form is the soul or principle of life. Further, you have argued that it is correct to assign primary causal responsibility to form in the explanation of a wide range of behaviors and changes that these natural beings undergo. So Aristotle argued in the sections of the *Physics* discussed in the preceding chapter. Imagine, in addition, that you have observed that these composite living beings are individual substances and that they are members of natural kinds, or species. We would leave something crucial out if we were simply to divide the natural world into two basic classes, souls and bodies, for example. Rather, these two factors combine, somehow, to produce a unified, determinate substance—a man or a horse. Further, these substances—men or horses—are the ontologically basic beings; all other beings inhere in them. So Aristotle argued in the passages from the *Metaphysics* discussed in Chapter 2. There is a tension between these two lines of thought because the analysis of composite substances into matter and form brings into question the role of sensible substances as the ontologically basic beings; and, for that reason, the status of sensible substances as substances is brought into question. For if they are composed of matter and form, one or both of these two components might seem to be more basic than the composites themselves. Another problem posed by the hylomorphic analysis of individual substances concerns the issue of their unity. What accounts for the unity of form and matter

---

[2]In *Metaphysics* VII–IX, Aristotle uses a number of words or phrases that together can be labeled his essentialist vocabulary: "essence" (τὸ τί ἦν εἶναι); a set of dative phrases, such as the "essence of man" (τὸ ἀνθρώπῳ εἶναι); and "form" (εἶδος) in contrast with the "material aspect" (ὕλη) of the composite substance. He distinguishes between two types of predication: in some predications, the thing predicated belongs to the subject *per se* (καθ' αὑτὸ); in others, the thing predicated belongs *per accidens* (κατα συμβεβηκός) to the subject. Aristotle explains these forms of predication in *Posterior Analytics* I.4; also see *Metaphysics* V.18 and the following note.

in the composite? Why is the composite substance one, a unity, rather than a multiplicity of beings? This question also poses a challenge to the claim of sensible or composite substances to be substances. For, as I explain below, Aristotle holds that substances are distinct from other beings by virtue of their high degree of unity.

I have sketched out the two constellations of ideas concerning indivdual substances and their hylomorphic analysis because it is primarily against this background, and in connection with these problems concerning the status of sensible substances, that Aristotle's notion of their essences in books vii– ix of the *Metaphysics* can be understood. On the one hand, essence is closely identified with form and formal cause, as playing the dominant role in the constitution of hylomorphic individual substances. Essence is the cause of being of sensible substances in that it causes them to be one. On this view, the notion of essence responds primarily to the difficulties concerning the unity of hylomorphic compounds. On the other hand, essence is characterized not as a unifying constituent of individual substances, but rather as a property (or properties) that both constitutes the species and belongs to the individual members of that species. An essential property is one that places the substance in a determinate kind. On this view, essence functions primarily to explain how composite substances are determinate individuals, i.e., individual members of species. As we shall see in Chapter 5, these alternative descriptions of the notion of essence and its functions help to generate a very difficult *aporia* concerning the appropriate way of characterizing the principles of substances. What is important to see at this point is that, on either story, Aristotle's description of what essence is and does is intimately connected with the final resolution of the population question. What Aristotle says about what essence is and does is inseparable from the issue of how it is that composite or material substances are substances.

It might seem that one way to reconcile the two ways of thinking about essences would be to hold that essence is both— that it is a unifying constituent of an individual substance *and* a special kind of property of them. Indeed, this picture, once articulated, appears quite reasonable, for it corresponds to a familiar way of thinking about essences: namely, that they are the necessary properties of objects. In this chapter, however, I argue that it is a mistake to think of an Aristotelian essence as a property of the substance whose essence it is. The reason an Aristotelian essence is not a property of the substance is a consequence of the role played by essence in the metaphysical theory of substance developed in the central books of the *Metaphysics*. For, as I explain in § 4, since the essence is the cause of being of the substance, it cannot be a property of it.

The claim that Aristotelian essences are not properties of substances is surprising on two counts. First, it is common practice today to think of essences as made up of the necessary properties of entities (even if only to deny that there are any). Second, it is also commonly thought that the distinction between essential (necessary) and accidental properties originated with Aristotle. It is thought to be his distinction. So, before turning to the considerations that led me to conclude that Aristotelian essences are not the properties of substances, it is important to see why the distinction between essential and accidental properties has been thought to originate with Aristotle.

1. *Per Se* and *Per Accidens* Predication

One factor that favors thinking of Aristotle's essences as the necessary properties of substances is the way in which the notion of essence is introduced in *Metaphysics* VII. 4. For there Aristotle says:

> Since in the beginning we distinguished in how many ways we define substance, and since one of these seemed to be the essence, we must investigate this. And first let us say some things about it linguistically. The essence of each thing is what it is said to be *per se*. For being you is not being musical, since you are not *per se* musical. What, then, you are *per se* is your essence. [1029b13–16]

In these introductory, linguistic comments about essence, it is pretty clear that Aristotle is referring to a distinction found in the *Posterior Analytics* between *per se* and *per accidens* predications. I prefer to use the Latin equivalents of the Greek phrases in question because their standard translations in English ("essential" and "accidental") are quite misleading.[3] For, as I explain below, not all *per se* predications are predications of essence; the standard English translations suggest a mistaken equation.

In *Posterior Analytics* I.4, Aristotle distinguishes four kinds of *per se* predications; in one of them, the predicate states the definition, or part of the definition, of the subject (73a34–37). That this form of predication is the one relevant to the notion of essence comes as no surprise to those familiar with the *Topics*, where the definition is described as the "statement indicating the essence" (101b37; also 101b21, 103b9–10). It is natural to think of the predicates in these *per se* predications as referring to the essential properties of the entity referred to by the subject term. For example, it is natural to think of the predication "Animal belongs to man *per se*" as ascribing a definitional property to man. Further, since Aristotle is perfectly willing to express the relationship between an *individual* substance and *its* essence in terms of a *per se* predication, it is equally plausible to think of an individual's essence as consisting of its necessary properties.[4] Aristotle also says of these predications that the things predicated belong to their subjects

---

[3] I translate "καθ' αὐτό" as *per se* and "κατα συμβεβηκός" as *per accidens*. In the *Posterior Analytics*, Aristotle distinguishes four uses of *per se* (I.4.73a34–73b16). The first two are the most important for our immediate purpose because they involve the notion of definition: either the predicate belongs in the definition of the subject, or the subject belongs in the definition of the predicate. At the end of the chapter, Aristotle says that both these kinds of predications are necessary. The third use of *per se* refers to a kind of being: beings that are not said of a subject are called "*per se*." As we shall see later, substances meet this requirement and so are called *per se* beings (see note 8 below). The fourth use marks a causal connection between events. If one event occurs because of another, then the connection between the two events is *per se* and not *per accidens*, or coincidental.

[4] For examples of *per se* predications with individual subjects, see *Metaphysics* VII.4.1029b13–16 and *Metaphysics* V.18.1022a25–29.

necessarily (*An. Post.* 73b16–18). From this text in the *Posterior Analytics*, then, it might seem that Aristotle thinks of essences as being composed of the necessary properties of substances. And since Aristotle begins his chapter on essences in the *Metaphysics* by referring to the distinction between *per se* and *per accidens* predications, it might seem that he is still thinking of essences as the necessary properties of entities.

It is very clear, however, that Aristotle never thought of an essence as comprising *all* the necessary properties of an object. There are two clear pieces of evidence that not *all* necessary properties are included in an Aristotelian essence. For one thing, in *Metaphysics* VII.4 Aristotle limits the notion of *per se* predication appropriate to essence to the case in which the thing predicated is part of the definition of the subject.[5] Further, even in the *Topics*, Aristotle distinguishes between the definition, which states the essence, and the *proprium*. The *proprium* is a predicate that, in contrast to the definition, does not display the essence of the subject. But the *proprium* does indicate a property that belongs to the subject alone and necessarily.[6] Aristotle explains what counts as a *proprium* a follows:

> For example, it is a *proprium* of man to be capable of learning grammar; for if a certain being is a man, he is capable of learning grammar, and if he is capable of learning grammar, he is a man. For no one calls anything a *proprium* which can possibly belong to something else; for example, he does not say that sleep is a *proprium* of man, even though at one moment it might happen to belong to him only. [102a20–25]

[5]The other kind of necessary *per se* predications is that in which the subject is part of the definition of the thing predicated.
[6]I use the Latin translation of Aristotle's term "'ἴδιον'" because the standard English translation "property" is very misleading. The problem is that the *proprium* is a special kind of property. Initially, Aristotle divides the *proprium* into two kinds, one that indicates the essence and one that does not; but then he proposes to call the former kind the definition and to reserve the term *proprium* for the latter kind (101b19ff.). The *proprium* "being capable of learning grammar" belongs to all human beings necessarily. If something is a human being, then it is capable of learning grammar (and vice versa). The *proprium* is a necessary but nonessential property.

The distinction between the definition and the *proprium* appears to be based on the idea that an answer to the question "What is it?" will not simply consist of a list of the object's necessary properties. So what is needed is a distinction between predicates—between definitions (which state the essence of the object) and *propria* (which state the object's necessary, but nonessential, properties).

These distinctions suggest that an entity can have necessary properties that are not part of its essence. But if Aristotle's notion of essence is not based on the idea of an object's necessary properties, then what *is* it based on?

The crucial question for Aristotle in connection with essences is the definitional question. Aristotle does not ask "What are this object's necessary properties?" in order to determine the object's essence; rather, he asks "What is it?" and the appropriate answer to this question is the definition of the object. As we have seen, the close connection between definition and essence is expressed in the *Topics*, where definition is said to be "the statement indicating the essence." And the centrality of the notion of definition for Aristotelian essences is further demonstrated in *Metaphysics* vii.4, where the problem of which things have essences is approached through a consideration of which things have definitions. What counts as essential is determined by the notion of definition. Even given the distinction in Aristotle's thought between the essence (which is indicated by the definition) and necessary properties (which are not included in the essence), it does not follow that essences are not necessary properties of objects. For it could be that the definition of the object is given by referring to some of the object's necessary properties. If this were so, then even if Aristotle's essentialism were based on the idea of the object's definition, rather than on the idea of its necessary properties, it could still turn out that essences are composed of some of the object's necessary properties. One problem for this line of interpretation is to explain why some necessary properties count as essential and others do not.

My objection to this idea—that essence, though based on the definition of the object, turns out to be composed of some of the object's necessary properties—stems from another concern. I said earlier that an Aristotelian definition is explanatory: in order to say what an entity is, one must explain it by means of principles and causes. My difficulty with the proposed view is that it attributes to Aristotle the position that some of the object's necessary properties (i.e., its definitional properties) are its principles and causes. Given Aristotle's view of what it is to be a principle, and given his views on the priority of substances in relation to nonsubstances (i.e., properties), it is very unlikely that he thought any properties could be the cause or principle of a substance. I shall develop my interpretation of this crucial claim more fully in § 4 below.

Before doing so, however, we must continue to discuss some preliminary issues. One such issue, which I address in the next section, concerns a second surprising feature of Aristotle's discussion of essences in *Metaphysics* vii.4–5. (The first distinctive feature was the centrality of the notion of definition, rather than of the notion of necessary property.) What is unexpected in Aristotle's discussion is his extended consideration of the question of which things have essences. The fact that Aristotle raises this issue casts initial doubt on the idea that essences are composed of some of the necessary properties of objects. For if they were, then there would be no reason to raise the issue of which things have essences: anything that had a necessary property would have an essence. Another preliminary issue, which I address in § 3, concerns the question of what Aristotle means by calling essence the "cause of being" of the substance. Clarification of these issues will set the stage. I will then be able to explain why I think that an object's necessary properties could not perform this function and, hence, why an Aristotelian essence does not comprise the necessary properties of a substance or a subset of them.

2. Substances, Nonsubstances, and the Notion of Essence

Aristotle's introductory comments on the notion of essence in *Metaphysics* vii.4 describe a form of predication appropriate for talking about essences. One begins by predicating the definition. But, how ought one to answer the question "What is it?" What counts as a definition? An answer favored by Aristotle in many contexts is the definition by genus and differentia. In the predication "Callias is *per se* an animal," the genus, an element in the definition of man, is predicated of the subject. The property "being an animal" is both a necessary property of Callias and an essential property, since it is part of his definition.[7] The definition by genus and differentia places individuals into kinds; by singling out the common definitional properties of a number of individuals, it explains why they are all members of the same kind. Clearly, this notion of definition and the correlative notion of essence apply equally well to substances and to entities in the other categories of being. Qualities, quantities, and the rest fall under genera and have their appropriate differentiae. We find Aristotle using this essentialist framework in the *Topics*; there is no restriction of the notions genus, differentia, definition, or essence to the category of substance. Indeed, in chapter 9 Aristotle explicitly states that they are predicated of all ten categories, and he says that when one says of a white color that it is a color, one is predicating its genus of it (103b31–38).

It is surprising, then, to find Aristotle in the *Metaphysics*, shortly after the introductory remarks quoted above, questioning the idea that nonsubstances have essences at all. Initially,

---

[7]Does Aristotle think that individuals have definitions? The argument of *Metaphysics* vii.15 might indicate they do not. There Aristotle argues that a composite substance such as Callias is not definable, on two grounds: (i) because of his matter and (ii) because of his individuality. On the other hand, we know that individuals are the subjects of essential/definitional predications (see note 4 above). Further, consider the relationship between definition and essence in Aristotle's thought. If individuals did not have definitions at all, then neither would they have essences at all. But surely the individual members of Aristotelian species have their species' form or essence, and the correlated definition will apply. In light of this line of thought, how should we understand the argument of *Metaphysics* vii.15? I interpret Aristotle as arguing that no definition includes mention of an individual's matter, and that no definition applies uniquely to an individual—it is always potentially applicable to a range of individuals. In this sense, definition is always of the universal; it is composed of general terms. I discuss this issue further in Chapter 5 (§ 1).

he does so on the grounds that nonsubstances are compounds or, to use his own terminology, because they are not *per se* beings (1029b22–27).[8] They are compounds because, as Aristotle argues in book VII, chapter 1, each nonsubstance inheres in a substance. The object to be defined is a compound being— a nonsubstance-in-a-substance. Aristotle pursues this line of thought later in the chapter; he claims that only substances are primary and noncompound, and he concludes that only they have definitions and essences (1030a2–17). One might think, then, that Aristotle's revised position is that only substances have essences.

Quite typically, however, Aristotle immediately considers another possibility: namely, that the notion of definition, and by implication the notion of essence, has more than one meaning or application. Aristotle's ultimate comment in this section of text on the question of whether or not nonsubstances have essences describes two possibilities: "Clearly, then, definition is the formula of the essence, and essence either belongs to substances alone or chiefly and primarily and in the unqualified sense" (1031a10–14).

One point suggested by this discussion is a consequence of the wedge Aristotle drives between the idea of *per se* predication and the notion of essence. For there is no question in *Metaphysics* VII.4–5 that nonsubstances can be the subjects of *per se* predications, yet there is very serious question concerning whether or not they have definitions and essences in the strict sense (1029b22–1030a6). Or, to put the point another way, Aristotle is concerned to distinguish between substances and nonsubstances with regard to the issue of their definitions and essences, but not with regard to the issue of *per se* predications.

---

[8]Aristotle's *per se* idiom is confusing because it is complicated. In one use, Aristotle contrasts *per se* and *per accidens* predications. He also uses the phrase to describe a kind of being: *per se* being is contrasted with *per accidens* being, the being of compound entities (e.g., a white man). In *Metaphysics* V.7, Aristotle says there are as many kinds of *per se* being as there are categories of being; so, substances, qualities, and so on are all *per se* beings. The final complication comes in *Metaphysics* VII.1, where, as we have seen, Aristotle seems to reserve the title of *per se* being for substance alone, presumably because all nonsubstances inhere in substances. See note 3 above for more on this terminology.

And this fact—that Aristotle discriminates between the issue of what can be the subject of a *per se* predication and the issue of which things have essences in the strict sense—should make us wary of basing our understanding of Aristotle's essentialism entirely on the notion of *per se* predication.

Even more important, for the purposes of this chapter, is that the distinction in this discussion between those entities which have essences (or have them unqualifiedly) and those which do not (or have them qualifiedly) depends upon whether or not the definition is of a unified, *per se* being (1030b4–13). Aristotle's tendency to say that substances alone have essences (or have them unqualifiedly) turns on two features of substances. Essences are correlated with definitions, which are answers to the question "What is it?" and substances have priority with regard to that question. Also, definitions are of unified beings, and substances are more unified than other beings—they are *per se*, rather than compound, beings. The explanation for both of these features of substances turns on the considerations I discussed in Chapter 2—i.e., on the view that nonsubstances inhere in substances, and substances do not inhere in anything else. Substances, because they are the ontologically basic beings, are unified objects of definition; nonsubstances, because they inhere in substances, are compounds and have compound definitions. But, given this characterization of substances as the unified objects of definition, a problem arises for the sensible or material substances. How can composite substances, compounds of matter and form, satisfy the unity requirement? In other words, the unity requirement casts doubt on the claim of sensible or material substances to be substances. The unity requirement forces us to raise the population question anew. But this is just what we should expect, since Aristotle holds that a final answer to the population question ("Is *x* a substance?") follows an answer to the definitional question ("What is substance?"). If substances are unified beings (and this is part of what it is to be a substance), then sensible or material substances must be unified beings. And, given their hylomorphic, compound natures, Aristotle must explain the principle or cause of their unity.

3. Essence as the Cause of Being of Substances

In this section, I address two questions: (i) Why is there a question of the cause of being of sensible or material substances? and (ii) What does it mean to say that essence is the cause of being of sensible substances?

With regard to the first question, it is important to recall that Aristotle thinks substances are the ontologically basic beings; other beings inhere in them. But his hylomorphic analysis of sensible, material substances casts doubt on whether or not they could count as ontologically basic. First, consider the issue of unity. If a substance were itself a compound of a number of entities, then those entities would underlie the substance. There are two obvious ways in which a composite substance could be thought to be a compound of a number of entities: it could be thought of as compounded out of matter and form, or it could be thought of as compounded out of its material parts. On either scenario, however, it would be plausible to argue that the substance itself would no longer be ontologically basic. Substances would no longer constitute the ground floor of being. So, if sensible substances, compounds of matter and form, are to count as substances, Aristotle must provide some explanation of their unity, both the unity of matter and form and the unity of their material parts. In this section, in connection with Aristotle's position that its form or essence is the cause of being of a substance, I discuss his account of the unity of the material parts. I shall discuss Aristotle's explanation of the unity of matter and form in the composite substance in § 5.

Second, consider the issue of determinateness. Substances are determinate individuals (a horse, a human). Indeed, as we have just seen, substances have definitions and essences in the primary sense. But since sensible substances are compound beings, the origin or principle of their determinateness is not clear. If we draw together the issues of substantial unity (the unity of the matter) and substantial determinateness, we can rephrase Aristotle's question: Why does this matter constitute a determinate, unified individual—a substance—rather than an indeterminate multiplicity? An answer to this question is an answer to the question "Why is it a substance?" And the answer to that question will state its cause of being, i.e., what is responsible for its being a substance.

The preceding few paragraphs contain a sketch of why Aristotle thinks there is a question concerning the cause of being of composite substances, together with an explanation of the meaning of the phrase "cause of being." It is now time to turn to the text, and to Aristotle's discussion of the idea that its form or essence is the cause of being of a substance.

The central text is *Metaphysics* VII.17, where Aristotle says he intends to approach the investigation of substance (the definitional question) from a new angle. "Since, therefore, substance is a certain principle and cause," he says, "one must inquire [about it] from there" (1041a9–10). To ask a causal question, continues Aristotle, is to ask a question whose general form is "Why does one thing belong to another?" (1041a10–11). He adds that the fact (i.e., that the one thing in question does belong to the other) must be assumed (1041a15–20). Here are two of Aristotle's examples:

(A) Why is man an animal of such a kind?

(B) Why are these bricks and stones a house?

Each of these questions satisfies the general requirement governing "why" questions since, in each of them, one thing is predicated of another. But the similarity ends there. For question (A) seems to be of an entirely different kind from question (B). Question (A) asks why a property applies to a substance, whereas question (B) asks why some matter composes an object of a determinate kind. We will follow Aristotle and concentrate on questions of type (B).

Questions of type (B), which I call questions of "substantial determinateness," are answered by mentioning the appropriate cause. Consider two ways of understanding question (B):

(B1) What made these bricks and stones into a house?

(B2) Why do these bricks and stones constitute a house?

The first sort of question is one concerning the process of generation; and for that sort of question, Aristotle tells us, it is appropriate to mention one kind of cause, what first moved, i.e., the efficient cause of the generation (1041a31–32). But the question understood as (B2) is of another sort; it is not a question of becoming, Aristotle says, but of being. To answer the question of the being of a composite substance, one must mention the cause of its being. Aristotle refers to this cause as either the form or the essence.[9] In some cases (e.g., the house), Aristotle points out, the essence is the final cause, or purpose, of the thing. So, what makes these building materials constitute a house is that they constitute a shelter for humans (or whatever the appropriate specification of a house's function might be).

Let us consider Aristotle's explanation of another example, a man. Unlike the house, a man is a clear case of a natural substance. Aristotle says:

> Since we must have the being of the thing as something given, clearly what is sought is why the matter is something; such as, why are these materials a house? Because the essence of house is present. And why is this, or this body having this, a man? So that what is sought is the cause of the matter, but this is the form, in relation to which it [the matter] is something. This is the substance. [1041b4–9]

Let us assume the fact that the thing in question, say this body (or, as Aristotle adds, this sort of body), is a man. We know, from §2 above, that a given individual such as Socrates is a man *per se*. However, we also know that Socrates is a composite entity; he can be analyzed into two components—matter and form. Which of these two components determines Socrates' nature such that Socrates is a *man* and not, for example, a *body*

---

[9] He uses "essence" (τὸ τί ἦν εἶναι) at 1041a28 and 1041b6; "form" (εἶδos) at 1041b8.

of a certain sort? But now Aristotle's point is not clear, for he has not presented any argument that Socrates is not a body of a certain sort. Moreover, it is not clear why we cannot say that Socrates is both a man and a body of a certain sort. In particular, that might be true if what it is to be a man is to be a body of a certain sort. In order to see Aristotle's point clearly, it is important to remember the context and purpose of his discussion. We have to remember that, for Aristotle, substances are the ontologically basic beings; thus, to say that Socrates is a body of a certain sort would be to say that a body (matter), rather than a composite (the man), is ontologically basic, is the substance. Aristotle does not argue this point because it has been assumed that sensible substances are substances. What he is trying to do in this passage is to explain *how it is* that they are substances. Aristotle's strongest line of argument against a materialist reduction (i.e., against the claim that matter is substance) is to be found, as I said in Chapter 3, in his arguments and considerations for teleology.

One important issue concerning Aristotle's hylomorphic analysis of sensible substances concerns how precisely to think of the contrast between form and matter. We can think of the contrast between building materials and a pile of them that constitutes a house quite easily. In living beings, the distinction between form and matter is far more subtle and complex, but there is no doubt that Aristotle considers the cases parallel to some degree. He contrasts a living human being and a corpse (*Parts An.* 640b34ff., 641a18ff.). In one case, the matter constitutes a human being; in the other, it does not. The difference is whether or not the soul is present. So much is clear, but we might still want to know exactly how Aristotle specifies matter and form in natural substances, as well as how matter and form are related to one another. I address these issues in the next section.

In *Metaphysics* VII.17, Aristotle also explains how the form or essence provides a solution to the problem of substantial unity. A human being is a unified entity over and above the sum of its parts. Socrates is a single being comprising (somehow) a number of organs—head, heart, hand—but Socrates is not simply the sum of his matter. Why is the composite substance itself not a heap of bodily organs, but a unified whole? Aristotle tries to answer this question by likening the composite substance to a paradigmatic non-heap, the syllable (1041b11ff.). He says: "Now the syllable is not the letters; 'B' and 'A' are not the same as 'BA.' . . . The syllable, therefore, is something, not only the letters, the vowels, and the consonants, but also something else" (1041b12–17). The relationship between the substance and what it is composed of is likened to the relationship between a syllable and the letters that compose it. First point of comparison: The syllable is not identical to the sum of its letters; just so, the composite substance is not identical to the matter that composes it. Second point of comparison: The syllable and the composite are unities, not heaps. Problem: What is the cause of their unity?

One might think that what causes the unity is just another material element: in the case of a syllable, another letter; in the case of a composite such as flesh, another material element added to the fire and earth that compose flesh. But we still have to ask what makes these elements one? Aristotle considers one other logical possibility: What if the cause of unity is itself a compound, rather than an element? If the cause of unity is a compound, however, then we can ask about the cause of *its* unity, and a regressive argument is generated. Aristotle concludes: "But it would seem that this is something and not an element, and it is the cause of being [which makes] this flesh and that a syllable. And similarly in all other cases. This is the substance of each thing (for this is the first cause of its being)" (1041b25–28). Although Aristotle does not mention form or essence in this resolution of the unity problem, his terminology strongly suggests that he intends to refer to form or essence. Two features of Aristotle's terminology require clarification in order for his intention to emerge. In the first place, Aristotle refers to the cause of being as the "substance of each thing," and this comes as a surprise because we had been thinking of form or essence as the cause of being. What is important to understand is that by the phrase "substance of each thing" Aristotle is referring to form or essence. Often, when he refers to form or essence as "substance," he should be understood as meaning the "substance of a substance"—in this case, a sensible substance. For example, in his discussion of the different things called "substance," Aristotle lists "that which, being present in such things as are not predicated of a subject, is the cause of their being, as the soul is the cause of being of animals" (1017b14–16).

The second point requiring clarification concerns what Aristotle means by saying that the cause of being is not an element. What contrast does he have in mind? His idea is to contrast material elements of things with their cause or principle—the form or essence.

Although there can be no doubt concerning the importance of the idea that substances are unified beings for Aristotle, it is not yet clear what notion of unity, of being one, is at issue here. Consider the example of the heap. Surely some notion of unity is applicable to a heap, a pile of stones. After all, we can count piles of stones. Aristotle does recognize as basic the notion of unity associated with counting and measurement; still, other senses of the term seem more appropriate for the discussion at hand.[10] Typically, Aristotle's discussions of the notion of unity are complex; there are different ways in which things are one, different degrees of unity. If we were to ask about the unity of the matter that composes a pile of stones, or of the matter that composes a person, for example, Aristotle would invoke the idea of the continuous to explain why we call each of these a unity: "There is the continuous, either in general or, especially, that which is continuous by nature and not by contact or by being tied together" (1052a18–20). According to this criterion of continuity, it would seem, the totality of the parts of the body compose one thing to a greater degree than either the stones in a heap or the stones in a wall; for the bodily parts are continuous by nature, rather than

---

[10]There are two extended discussions of "unity" in the *Metaphysics* (v.6 and x.1). In both texts, Aristotle emphasizes the notion of a "measure" as central to unity (1016b17ff., 1052b18ff.). "Measure" is not the most important concept for our purposes, however, since Aristotle says that it originates in, and most properly applies to, the category of quantity.

merely by contact or by being bound together. Aristotle also says that the things that are continuous by nature have "one movement" (1016a5, 1052a20–21). Again, it would seem that the totality of the parts of an animal could satisfy this requirement, whereas it is doubtful whether the stones that compose a pile could. Each stone has a single motion (i.e., to move down), but the pile need not have one motion. The case of the body is different: each part has a motion, but so does the body as a whole. It is fair to conclude, then, that the parts of a body are more unified than the stones in a pile. Later I shall discuss how this ranking according to the continuity criterion is related to the issue of substantial unity. It will turn out that the priority with respect to unity of bodies over piles of stones is a consequence of the fact that the bodies constitute substances.

Aristotle's present concern is with substantial unity—the unity of an animal, not of an animal's body—a kind of unity, he thinks, that heaps such as a pile of stones entirely lack. For, as we have seen, Aristotle makes a distinction between the material that composes a substance and the composite substance itself. So, in the case of a substance, to explain the unity of its matter does not accomplish the task of explaining the unity of the substance; for a nonsubstantial heap, on the other hand, the only unity that requires explaining is the weak degree of unity of its matter. A heap of stones is a unity just insofar as the stones are in contact; for an animal to be a unity, however, more than just the continuity of the body is involved.

In general, then, a more rigorous notion of unity applies to substances, and that notion is not equivalent to mere continuity in either of its senses:

> While in a sense we call anything one if it is a quantity and continuous, in a sense we do not unless it is a whole, i.e., unless it has unity of form; e.g., if we saw the parts of a shoe put together anyhow, we should not call them one all the same (unless because of their continuity); we do this only if they are put together so as to be a shoe and to have already a certain single form [1016b12–16; also see 1052a21–25]

Even if the parts of an entity are continuous, and there is a sense in which it is appropriate to call them "one," there is another sense in which the term does not apply unless the entity has a single form. This point is easiest to illustrate with an artifact, in the way that Aristotle does in the text just quoted. We can imagine the parts of a shoe being continuous but misplaced so that they do not function as a shoe, which is just to say that the object lacks the shoe form or essence. Similarly, continuity of a human being's material parts is not sufficient to explain the unity of the human being; for that, the parts have to be continuous in a way that makes them capable of functioning humanly. But it is the presence of soul that accomplishes this. Living natural beings are different from artifacts such as shoes in that what is required for them to be able to function is more than just the correct arrangement of the parts. The parts of a corpse might be continuous and arranged in the right way, yet they are not capable of functioning humanly. The matter of a corpse has the same sort of low-grade unity that attaches to piles of stones.

It is worthwhile to return for a moment to the "one movement" criterion that, Aristotle says, discriminates between those things which are naturally continuous and those which are not. I suggested that the matter of a composite substance (e.g., a body) meets this criterion, whereas the stones in a heap do not. You might think that the body (or matter) has "one movement" quite independent of the soul (or form), and that the fact that the body is "more one" than the stones is entirely independent of the issue of substantial unity. A moment's reflection on the difference between corpses and living animals, however, will convince us that this is not so. For Aristotle does not think that the body alone is causally responsible for the animal's movement. In his view, it is the form that causes the body to have one movement (whether that movement be locomotion, growth, or reproduction). The body has one movement not by itself, but by virtue of the soul. The two criteria for unity that we have considered are not completely independent: the high degree of unity by continuity of the matter in the case of animals, in contrast with stones in a pile, is a consequence of the fact that the matter in question is the matter of an animal, a composite substance.

We are now in a position to bring together a number of themes from this chapter, and then to proceed to consider whether or not an Aristotelian essence is a necessary property of a substance. We saw in § 2 that Aristotle vacillates between saying (i) that only substances have definitions and essences and (ii) that substances have definitions and essences in the unqualified sense, but nonsubstances also have them in a qualified sense. Both these options are based on the idea that substances are unified beings, whereas nonsubstances are compound beings. But the fact that composite substances are material threatens their unity from below and, hence, poses a threat to their claim to be substances. Aristotle fends off this threat by claiming that its form or essence is responsible for the matter constituting a unified determinate being, rather than a heap. Viewed from this perspective, essence is the cause of being of a substance in that it causes it to be a substance: namely, a unified determinate being, an individual. In this connection, we can understand Aristotle's remarks that only those beings with definitions (in the unqualified sense) will have essences (in the unqualified sense) and, further, his claim that only substances have definitions and essences (in the unqualified sense). For the question of which beings have definitions and essences is ultimately a question of their unity. As we have seen, moreover, Aristotle tries to make the case that composite substances have more unity than either nonsubstances or matter. But if they have more unity, then that is just to say that they have essences, for essences are causes and principles of unity; and to say that they have essences is just to say that they have definitions, for definitions are just "statements which indicate the essence." Once we understand that essence is a principle of unity, as well as a principle of determination, we can also understand Aristotle's vacillation on the issue of whether or not essences should be restricted to substances. For it makes sense to think of unity in two ways. We can establish a criterion of unity, say the unity of substances, and deny that anything that does not meet that criterion is unified. According to this way of thinking, only substances will have essences. On the other hand—by holding that the most unified beings have essences in an unqualified sense, while allowing that other beings have them in a qualified sense—we can think of unity as a matter of degree. According to this approach, substances will have essences in an unqualified sense, but nonsubstances will have them in a qualified sense.

4. The Relationship between Essence and Composite Substance

What has any of this to do with my opening claim that an Aristotelian essence is not a property of the substance? In the passage of the *Metaphysics* I discussed in the preceding section, Aristotle proposes an analysis of the being of individual, composite substances; he says that form or essence is the cause or principle of being of an individual substance. For example, the soul is the cause of being of a human being; it is the presence of soul that causes some matter (this flesh and bone) to constitute an actual human being. And it is the actual human being that is ontologically basic and the subject of *per se* and *per accidens* predications: "Socrates is a man *per se*" and "Socrates is pale *per accidens*." Aristotle's analysis can be shown as follows:

Soul (Essence or Form) + Body (Matter) > Socrates > is a man
                                                          is pale
                                                          etc.

My claim is that form or essence is not a property of the individual composite substance because Aristotle identifies form or essence as the cause of being of an individual substance. But why does it follow, from the function I ascribe to essence in Aristotle's explanation of composite substances, that essence is not a property of the individual substance? Why cannot one or more of its properties be its cause of being?

Consider any individual substance *a* and any property *F*. Is it possible to explain why *a* is an actual individual substance by predicating *F* of *a*? Could the possession of a property by an individual substance ("*a* being *F*") constitute an adequate explanation or analysis of what makes this matter constitute *a*? It is quite clear that this explanation is unsatisfactory because it is circular. For the proposed answer to the question "Why is this matter *a*?"—namely, "*a* being *F*"—includes mention of *a*. Imagine pointing to an actual individual substance and asking Aristotle's question: "Why is this matter a substance?" The answer "because it is an individual substance with a certain property" employs the notion of an individual substance in what was supposed to be an explanation of the being of that individual substance.

A critic might object as follows. Even if I accept your argument that it would be circular to cite a property of an actual substance as its cause of being, it still does not follow that the essence or cause of being is not a property of the substance. Consider the house example. True, in response to the question "Why do these bricks and stones constitute a house?" it would be circular to say "because the house is a shelter for humans." Rather, as you point out, it is the presence of essence or form to the matter that constitutes the actual individual house. But is not the form or essence—in this case, the functional property "being a shelter for humans"—a property? Indeed, is it not a necessary and essential property of the house? In short, the objection is this: although the actual substance having a certain property cannot be the cause of being of the substance, its cause of being can nonetheless be one of its properties.

Not for Aristotle. To understand why Aristotle would not accept the idea that the cause of being of a substance might be one of its properties, it is helpful to recall a point from Chapter 2. There I explained Aristotle's view that anything predicated of a substance, any nonsubstance, has an individual substance as *its* cause of being. So, translating the proposed view into Aristotle's terminology, we can say that the actual individual substance would be both the cause of being and prior to what is predicated of it, and that at least some of what is predicated of it would be both prior to and the cause of being of the substance. That Aristotle would not accept this account is clear on two grounds:

(i) It is internally inconsistent, in that the cause of being of the substance is both prior to and posterior to it. A necessary property of a substance, if it is essential, is on Aristotle's view the cause of being of the substance; hence, it is prior to it. On the other hand, the necessary property, *qua* property, has as its cause of being the individual substance and is posterior to it.

(ii) It contravenes a central Aristotelian doctrine—namely, the priority of substances—which is to be found in early works such as the *Categories* and in mature works such as the *Metaphysics*. If one or more of its properties were the cause of being of a substance, then they would also be prior to the substance.

My argument rests on the idea that if one thing is the cause of being of another, then it is prior to it. Point (ii), for example, says that if one of its properties were the cause of being of a substance, then one of its properties would be prior to it. This idea raises two questions. First, why think that Aristotle made the connection I suggest between the notions "cause of being" and "priority." Second, what do I mean by "prior" in this context? The question of the meaning of "priority" is crucial to point (i) above, since the internal inconsistency I describe would be avoided if substances and properties were prior to one another in different senses. A substance could be onto-logically, but not epistemologically, prior to its properties.

Aristotle lists possible uses of "priority" and "posteriority" in several places;[11] but, for our purposes, and in relation to the texts and issues that we have been considering, the most important text is the one I explained at some length in Chapter 2. The text is from the opening chapter of Aristotle's investigation of the notion of substance: "Now there are several senses in which a thing is said to be primary; but substance is primary in every sense—in formula, in knowledge, in time" (1028a31–33). As I explained in Chapter 2, these three kinds of priority are the priorities that Aristotle assigns to those beings which

[11]In *Metaphysics* v.11, for example, there is a lengthy discussion of the terms "prior" and "posterior."

are ontologically basic. So, if one being is prior to another being according to these three kinds of priority, then the former is an ontologically basic being and the latter is not. If a substance is prior to its properties, then it is the ontologically basic being, and its properties are not. On the other hand, if some of its properties are prior to a substance, then they are ontologically basic and the substance is not. Given this understanding of the notion of priority, it is easy to see that it would be inconsistent to hold that a substance is prior to its properties and that some of its properties are prior to it. And, the threefold priority of substances in relation to attributes includes both ontological and epistemological priority, so it precludes the possibility of holding that a substance is ontologically prior to its properties, but that its properties are epistemologically prior to the substance.[12]

What evidence do we have that Aristotle thought that if a being were the cause of being of another, then the former would be prior (in the sense just explained) to the latter? In *Metaphysics* VII.1, the chapter in which Aristotle explains the threefold priority of substance, he also says that nonsubstances are because of substances.[13] And that is just another way of saying that substances are the cause of being of nonsubstances. Indeed, that substances play this role is the reason Aristotle gives for calling them "primary being," which in turn motivates

[12]The threefold priority of substances (discussed in Chapter 2, § 3) holds between substances and attributes. In the case of substances and attributes it is not possible to drive a wedge between their ontological and epistemological relations. But what about substances and universals? Could individual substances not be prior to universals ontologically, and universals be prior to individual substances epistemologically? If so, then an individual substance could have a universal epistemological principle that is prior to it, and one of its causes. Certainly, this is a possible position, but we do not find Aristotle adopting it. Moreover, in the text in which all the ingredients for distinguishing ontological and epistemological priority are present, Aristotle fails to make the distinction. Instead, he demotes the epistemological priority of the universal in relation to the individual substance by claiming that actual knowledge is of the individual (*Metaph.* XIII.10). See Chapter 5 (§ 3) for a discussion of this text.

[13]"It is clear, then, that it is on account of this [substance] that each of the others [attributes] is" (1028a29–30). In other words, substance is the cause of being of attributes.

his subsequent explanation of the three ways in which one thing can be prior to another (1028a29–34). The connection between the notion of priority and the notion that one thing is the cause of being of another can also be seen in this discussion of several senses of "prior" from the *Categories*: "There are, then, these many ways of speaking of the prior. There would seem, however, to be another manner of priority besides those mentioned. For of things which reciprocate as to implication of being, that which is in some way the cause of another's being might reasonably be called prior by nature" (14b10–13).

My argument is intended to show why it is a mistake to think of an Aristotelian essence as a property of the substance. According to Aristotle, what it means to be an actual individual substance is that a form or essence is present in some matter. And this position suggests not that the form or essence is a property of the composite substance, but rather that it is a property of the matter. Indeed, Aristotle seems to express this view in several texts where he states explicitly that form is predicated of matter (*Metaphysics* VII.3.1029a23–24, IX.7.1049a34–b6, VII.13.1038b5). I discuss these texts, as well as Aristotle's account of the relationship between form and matter, in the next section.

First, though, let us consider one difference between Aristotle's theory of essences—according to which essences are not the properties of the objects of which they are the essences—and an essentialism according to which essences are the necessary properties of objects. The fundamental difference concerns what it is that essences are supposed to explain. An essentialist theory which holds that essences are the necessary properties of objects does not, and does not intend to, provide an account of the cause of being of individual substances. Instead, it raises a different question about individual substances: it asks, *of* an individual substance, what it is to be that substance. And the answer is, roughly, that any thing (any individual) with property *x* or properties *x, y*, etc. is that substance. On this theory of essences, an essential property is one that an individual object must have in order to be that very object. Essential properties are based upon the identity of an individual substance; they are those properties which anything which is that object must have. Aristotle's notion of form or essence is meant to explain why there is an individual substance there at all, not what features constitute the identity of a given individual substance within a domain of individual substances. I explore additional points of divergence and contact between Aristotle's essentialism and Saul Kripke's version of contemporary essentialism in Chapter 6.

5. The Relationship between Form or Essence and Matter

An important theme of the present chapter is (i) that Aristotle faces serious problems with respect to the unity of composite substances and (ii) that, since unity is a mark of substance, there is a question whether or not they should count as substances at all. Their unity is threatened from two directions. For one thing, since they are material substances, there is a question concerning how their matter is unified into an individual substance. In § 3, I presented Aristotle's position that its form or essence is responsible for the fact that its matter constitutes an individual substance. The other threat to the unity of composite substances arises from the fact that they are compounds of form (or essence) and matter. How are form and matter related to one another so that what results is a unified being, a substance?

Let us consider some possibilities. If one held that matter and form were themselves independent substances, then the composite substance would not be a basic unity. And if it is not a basic unity, then it would not be a substance—it would be at best a union of two substances. Since Aristotle's purpose is to explain *how it is* that sensible or composite substances are substances, it seems that we should not think of matter and form as independent substances. Another possible way of thinking of their relationship is to think of the form or essence as a property of the matter. This interpretation is attractive for two reasons. First, it avoids the "two substances" problem: if we think of the form or essence as a property of the matter, then clearly form or essence is not a substance. On this view, form or essence could not be a substance, since the form or essence would not be ontologically basic and (as we saw in Chapter 2) to be ontologically basic is a central characteristic of substances. For to say that form is a property of matter means that it has matter as its subject, which is just to say that form is not ontologically basic. Second, as I remarked in § 4, there seems to be textual support for this view. The most explicit statements that Aristotle makes concerning the unity of matter and form, however, employ the concepts of potentiality and actuality. For example: "Therefore, to ask the cause of their [i.e., matter and form] being one is like asking the cause of unity in general; for each thing is a unity, and the potential and the actual are somehow one" (VIII.6.1045b19–21). This comment suggests a third understanding of the relationship between matter and form, one in which matter is potentiality and form is actuality. In the remainder of the present chapter, I develop this third possible interpretation. I explain that potentiality and actuality should be understood as ways of being, and I show how the "ways of being" interpretation solves the problem of the unity of the composite substance. By way of setting the stage, however, let us first sketch out the second possible interpretation, consider the texts that favor it, and point out its very serious drawbacks.

Is Socrates' soul a property of his body? And if form or essence *is* a property of the matter, then how should we understand this relationship? The most important support for those who would answer "yes" to the question leading off this paragraph consists of several texts in which Aristotle says that form is predicated of matter: "Whenever this is so, then the ultimate subject is a substance; but when this is not so, but the thing predicated is a form and an individual, the ultimate subject is matter and material substance" (IX.7.1049a34–36; cf. VII.3.1029a23–24, 10.1038b4–6). These texts suggest a two-tier ontology: nonsubstances are predicated of substance; and, at bottom, form is predicated of matter. But what is the correct understanding of the relationship between the two tiers? According to the proposed interpretation, Aristotle is telling us in these passages that we should understand the relation between matter and form as parallel to the relation between substance and nonsubstance. In other words, form or essence is an accidental property of matter, just as a nonsubstance is an accidental property of a substance. The bottom tier mirrors the top tier. On this view, form is an accident or property of matter, and the substance is an accidental unity of form and matter.[14]

The difficulty with this interpretation is that it treats a substance as an accidental unity having the same logical structure as the accidental unity of a property and a substance (e.g., a quality and a substance). In his discussion of "unity" in *Metaphysics* v.6, however, Aristotle clearly differentiates between those things which are "one" accidentally and those which are "one" by their own nature (1015b16–17). And in his discussion of accidental unity, Aristotle includes examples of substances and properties (e.g., "musical Coriscus" [1015b17]), whereas he discusses things unified by form under the other division (those things which are one by their own nature [1016b12–18]). This all makes perfect sense if we recall that substances are highly unified beings, so that the relationship between form and matter could not be parallel to that between substance and accident. How could Socrates be a *per se* being if his form and matter were related as an accidental property is to its subject—if Socrates were a "bundle"?

Thus far, I have argued that form or essence is not a property of matter in the way that an accident is a property of a substance. So, to return to the texts cited above, whatever Aristotle means by saying form is predicated of matter, he does *not* mean that form is an accidental property of matter. On the other hand, it is fairly obvious that form cannot be an essential or necessary property of the matter. Wood is not necessarily a table; after all, it might have been a hatrack. Form is not an

---

[14]I used to hold this view myself. See "Form, Reproduction, and Inherited Characteristics in Aristotle's *Generation of Animals*," *Phronesis*, 30 (1985), note 17.

accidental property of matter, and it is not a necessary property of matter.[15] These considerations, I believe, make it unlikely that Aristotle holds form or essence to be a property of matter in the composite substance. Aristotle says that the difficulty of explaining the unity of the composite is eased once we grasp the notion that form and matter are to one another as actuality is to potentiality. It makes sense, therefore, to try to understand actuality, potentiality, and the relationship between them with respect to the question of the unity of the composite substance.

What does Aristotle mean by "actuality" and "potentiality"? In the discussion of "being" in *Metaphysics* v.7, the distinction between actual and potential being is presented last. Aristotle tells us that the distinction applies to the other three divisions of being: *per se* being, *per accidens* being, and being as true or false (1017a35). To see what Aristotle might have in mind, let us consider *per se* being. *Per se* being is mapped out by categorical predications: e.g., "Socrates is a human being." If we apply the distinction between potential and actual being to the categorical predication, we get "Socrates is potentially a human being" and "Socrates is actually a human being." But what does it mean to say that something is potentially a human being? Is it a human being or not? And what does it mean to say that something is actually a human being? How does that assertion differ from simply saying that something *is* a human being?

In the text we are considering, Aristotle illustrates the potentiality/actuality distinction as follows:

---

[15]There is another possibility. Imagine the process by which a table is made. There is a series of accidental changes in the matter which, at some point, becomes a table; i.e., the matter acquires the form of a table. The form of a table is a property of the matter that "supervenes" on it after a series of changes in the accidental properties of the wood. Once the wood has been altered such that it can function as a table, the form or essence (for Aristotle, specified in functional terms) is a property of the wood-of-the-right-shape. The advantage of this account is that the functional property is not an accidental property of the wood-of-the-right-shape, but rather a necessary one, and so the resulting object, the table, is not merely accidentally one. But if the functional property were a necessary property of the wood-of-the-right-shape, that wood would just be a table; and, if it were, then the wood-of-the-right-shape is the composite itself and not the matter.

> For we say both of that which sees potentially and of that which
> sees actually, that it is seeing; and both of that which can use
> knowledge and of that which is using it, that it knows; and both
> of that to which rest is already present and of that which can
> rest, that it rests. And similarly, in the case of substances, we
> say that Hermes is in the stone, and the half of the line is in
> the line, and we say of that which is not yet ripe that it is corn.
> [1017b2-9]

The first set of contrasts is between a capacity and its exercise.
A person who has knowledge has a certain capacity. In relation
to the exercise of that knowledge, the person is a potential
knower. Here, the person who is an actual knower is a person
exercising that capacity. Let us group together these sorts of
examples of potentiality and actuality under the label *capacity
and exercise* (CE for short). In relation to these examples, what
we mean when we say "Socrates is actually a human being"
is that he is exercising his capacity for being human. He is in
action.

Aristotle next lists several examples of substances: e.g., unripe corn is potentially corn; when it ripens, it is actually corn.
This example invites us to think not of a capacity and its exercise, but of a continuum of directed development. Unripe
corn is corn potentially—it is in process toward its end, which
is being corn actually. Mature corn is corn actually—it has
achieved its end. These examples of potentiality and actuality
can be grouped together under the label *process and end* (PE for
short). In relation to these examples, what we mean when we
say "Socrates is actually a human being" is that Socrates has
fully achieved that set of capacities which a mature human
being has. Of the youthful Socrates, the Socrates who lacks the
capacity to theorize, we would say "Socrates is potentially a
human being."[16]

---

[16]In *Metaphysics* ix, Aristotle's explanation of the meaning of potentiality and
actuality in connection with being and substance also proceeds by way of
example (1048a30–b9). Aristotle lists four examples of the CE class and four
examples of the PE type. Aristotle summarizes as follows: "But all things are
not said in the same sense to exist actually, but only by analogy—as *A* is in *B*
or to *B*, *C* is in *D* or to *D*; for some are as movement to potentiality, and the
others as substances to some sort of matter" (1048b6–9). The two sorts of

It is interesting that in our text Aristotle stresses the similarity of the PE examples to the CE examples, rather than their differences (1017b6). How is the relationship between unripe corn and mature corn like the relationship between a capacity and its exercise? In order to see the similarity, we must distinguish two capacities of the corn: the capacity for becoming corn and the capacity for being corn. The capacity for becoming corn is the capacity the seedling has to grow, develop, and ripen. The capacity to develop into ripe corn is a capacity that the seedling has only so long as it is potentially, and not actually, ripe. The potentiality for becoming corn is used up in the corn's development. Hence, the potentiality for becoming corn differs importantly from the relationship between a capacity and its exercise. The potentiality for becoming corn perishes as the seedling ripens, but a person retains the capacity for sight even while he or she is seeing. This point suggests that Aristotle is thinking rather about the seedling's capacity for being corn. The seedling's capacity for being (ripe) corn is a potentiality the corn has to achieve its end. This capacity is exercised when the corn is ripe and mature, just as a person's capacity for sight is exercised when he or she sees. The cases are similar because in neither is the capacity used up in the exercise. Just as a person can see when he or she is seeing, so, too, the corn can continue to be corn while it is corn. These observations suggest that there is a difference between potentiality and actuality as they are used in connection with being and as they are used in connection with the analysis of changes or motions that entities undergo. It is not the motion of ripening that Aristotle is trying to explain by contrasting unripe and ripe corn, calling one "potential" and the other "actual," but different ways of being corn. This is an important point because potentiality and actuality do figure centrally in Aristotle's

---

potentiality and actuality, the one associated with motion and the other associated with being and substance, are similar to one another; they are the same by analogy. As I understand this text, the examples that Aristotle has listed, the four CE and four PE examples, are all examples of the kind of potentiality and actuality associated with substance. They exemplify a relationship between "substance and some sort of matter."

analysis of motion, and so it would be easy to misunderstand his purpose.[17]

If the ripening-corn example of potentiality and actuality is not understood in terms of an analysis of the motion of ripening, however, other questions arise concerning the meaning of the distinction. What does Aristotle mean by distinguishing different ways of being corn or being human? Why does he make this distinction? Why not stick to austere categorical being and say of the unripe corn and the child what we would say: namely, that it is corn or a human being?

The answer to this question is that Aristotle thinks of these sorts of beings—composite substances—as being en route or directed toward their respective ends. Beings that are en route are simply beings at different levels of potentiality or actuality. Here, again, it is important not to take Aristotle's point as being about the route, the series of motions that accomplish the perfection of the corn or the human. Rather, with the notions of potentiality and actuality, Aristotle expresses ontological relations among the beings at different stages, from a perspective in which all the stages are directed toward a series of ends. The phrase "directed toward a series of ends" is important. For, viewing the life of a human being as comprising a succession of stages—youth, middle age, old age—does not have any ontological implications. If all one means by saying that a youth is potentially middle aged is that the former stage precedes the

---

[17]That Aristotle treats "actuality" and "potentiality" in connection with being and substance as different from "actuality" and "potentiality" used in connection with motion is confirmed in Aristotle's opening remarks in *Metaphysics* IX.1: "First let us explain potentiality in the strictest sense, which is, however, not the most useful for our present purpose. For potentiality and actuality extend further than the mere sphere of motion" (1045b35–1046a1). And when Aristotle has finished explaining potentiality in relation to motion, he reiterates this point before embarking on his explanation of the other sense of potentiality and actuality (1048a25–30). L. A. Kosman, "Substance, Being, and *Energeia*," *Oxford Studies in Ancient Philosophy*, 2 (1984), 121–149, first drew my attention to the importance of these passages. My interpretation of the unity of composite substances differs from Kosman's on several points, the most important of which is that, on my view, Aristotle maintains a distinction between the proximate matter and the composite substance, whereas Kosman's Aristotle identifies the two.

latter, then a young person differs from an older person only by temporal position. On this view, the earlier stage is fully what it is quite independently of the later stage. For Aristotle, however, there is a connection between the stages because the *way* the entity is what it is in the earlier stage is determined by an actuality, a later stage. The stages are determined by the overall end of the progression. So, the youthful Socrates is potentially human, where what it is to be human is given in the final actuality, the activity of a mature human being. Beings such as Socrates (composite substances) are directed beings in the sense that what they are is determined by their ends, and they are en route toward their ends.

I said that the being of the entity in the earlier stage is *determined by* a correlated end. What sort of determination is in question here? In *Metaphysics* ix.9 Aristotle tells us that actuality is prior to potentiality in several ways. Two priorities, priority in being and priority in definition, are what I have in mind in saying that potential being is determined by actual being.

Concerning the priority in being of actuality in relation to potentiality, Aristotle says, "everything that comes to be moves toward a principle and end. For that for the sake of which a thing is is its principle, and the becoming is for the sake of the end" (1050a7–9). Beings that are en route exist toward their ends. They are for the sake of their ends. The principle of being for the youthful Socrates is an actuality (Socrates actively being human). But, in the young Socrates, the principle that governs his being, his form or end, is not actually or fully present. So the youthful Socrates is potentially human, precisely because his being is determined by an end or actuality that he has not yet achieved. Being potentially human is one way of being human, a way in which what you are is not yet realized; your principle or end is not yet realized in you. Being actually human is another way of being human, a way in which what you are (the principle of your being) is fully realized in you.

Actuality is also prior to potentiality in definition because a potentiality is defined in relation to its correlative actuality. For example, the capacity of sight is defined as being able to see, to engage in a certain activity (1049b13–15). Similarly, when we say what the youthful Socrates is, we say he is potentially human; he is potentially a being that engages in a certain characteristic range of activities. The priority of actuality over potentiality in definition is really a consequence of the priority in being. Since an Aristotelian definition says what a thing is, and since the principle of being of a potentiality is the corresponding actuality, it follows that the statement of what the potentiality is (its definition) will refer to the end or actuality.

Potential and actual being describe the ways in which things are what they are. In Aristotle's system, they are a necessary addition to the more familiar picture of categorical being, since they describe a basic feature of reality: namely, that it is directional. What something is is determined by its form and end, and by its relationship to that form and end. Potentiality and actuality admit of degrees because an end can be realized in different ways, i.e., to a greater or lesser extent.[18] Thus far in our discussion, the way of being of a substance—namely, the degree to which it has realized its form or end— has two basic varieties. The mature Socrates is fully in his form, and the immature Socrates is not. Socrates in action is more fully realizing his form than Socrates asleep.

Before I turn to the application of these notions to the relationship between matter and form in the composite substance, I want to connect this discussion with a point made at the end of the preceding chapter. There I said that Aristotle's notion of the form or essence of natural beings is inherently teleological. By this I meant that Aristotle's defense of teleology constitutes his defense of the primacy of form for the understanding of natural beings, and that Aristotle considers

[18]One of the distinguishing characteristics of substance in the *Categories* is that it does *not* admit of degrees. How does this comment cohere with the idea that substances can be more or less actualized? In *Metaphysics* VIII.3, Aristotle says the following: "And as number does not admit of the more and the less, neither does substance in the sense of form, but if any substance does, it is only the substance which involves matter" (1044a9–11). Substances that do not involve matter are presumably fully actual.

the form of natural beings to be a kind of goal or end. The explanation I have just given concerning what Aristotle means by potential being and actual being should reinforce the picture of forms or essences as ends or goals. Composite substances are beings en route: they are directed toward their forms or essences.

In my Socrates example, I have been thinking of a human being as existing in different ways, at various degrees of actuality. Human beings, sensible substances, have this sort of being because they are composites of matter and form: "Further, matter exists in a potential state, just because it may attain to its form; and when it exists actually, then it is in its form" (1050a15–16). Underlying the process of the composite substance realizing its form more and more is matter, which at one moment "may attain to its form" and at another moment is "in its form."[19] Even when matter is in its form, however, the composite substance has two aspects, two ways of being. One is potential being, associated with matter; the other is actual being, associated with form. If it did not have these two aspects, it would not be a being capable of degrees of actualization. Nor could it be a being that lives and dies. But how ought we think about this fundamental duality of aspect in the composite? And how does it mesh with the other applications of potentiality and actuality? What kind of unity results?

What we are looking for is a level of potentiality and actuality, corresponding to matter and form, that underlies and makes possible PE and CE potentiality and actuality. And we find just such a level of potentiality and actuality in Aristotle's discussion of the soul in the *De Anima*. For Aristotle, a human being's form is his or her soul, and in the *De Anima* soul is defined as "the first actuality of a natural body that has life potentially" (412a20–21). The matter of an ensouled entity is "a natural body that has life potentially"; the matter of a human being is a

---

[19]The text just quoted in note 18 confirms the role of matter as underlying the processes of actualization in the composite. It is because the composite has matter that it admits of more or less—that it can be actualized to varying degrees.

natural body that has human life potentially. Form or soul is the first grade of actuality that corresponds to the capacity for life (in our example, for human life). A composite substance such as a human being has two ways of being; its matter is a body that is potentially alive, and its form is a soul or a set of capacities that constitute human life. The set of capacities for life (and the exercise of those capacities) is, of course, an example of CE potentiality and actuality. Further, these human capacities are developed throughout life, from the immature specimen of a human being to a mature exemplar; a child can neither reproduce itself nor theorize. This development, which I have called PE potentiality and actuality, is possible because one aspect of the composite which is material (potential) has a potentiality for those capacities whose principle is soul or form. If the matter did not have the right set of potentialities, then the process of maturity or actualization would not occur. Aristotle stresses this point in his reflections in *Metaphysics* viii–ix concerning the proximate matter. On the other hand, if the composite did not retain its potentiality (its being as matter), then there would be no *process* of maturity, no gaps in activity, no eventual death, and, of course, no problem of unity. As Aristotle says, "And all things which have no matter are without qualification essentially unities" (viii.6.1045b23–24).

The relationship between form and matter, or soul and body, does not appear to be identical to either CE or PE potentiality and actuality as I have described them. We cannot liken the body to a capacity and the soul to its exercise, for soul is clearly described by Aristotle as a first actuality of the body, i.e., a set of capacities rather than their exercise. Soul is that aspect of the composite which causes it to be alive, to be able to do a number of things, to grow or perceive or reproduce. But the matter, Aristotle says, is only potentially alive; it is the capacity for the capacity to live. If this is so, however, then one cannot think of matter and form in the composite on our other model, either. For in PE potentiality and actuality, the potential being is eventually the actual being; i.e., at some point the unripe corn is ripe. According to Aristotle's specification of the body as "potentially alive," the difference between the two cases is that the matter itself is never actually alive—its potentiality for life is retained.[20]

Aristotle is not unaware of a third sort of potentiality and actuality, however, for in the *De Anima* he illustrates this level of potentiality (the capacity for a capacity) with the example of a knower:

[20]An important challenge to my view—that the matter in a composite is always only potentially enformed—is developed in John Ackrill, "Aristotle's Definitions of psuchê," in *Articles on Aristotle 4. Psychology and Aesthetics*, ed. Jonathan Barnes, Malcolm Schofield, and Richard Sorabji (New York: St. Martin's Press, 1979), pp. 65–75. Ackrill argues that the proximate matter of a human being, organic parts such as heart and hand, are always necessarily enformed. If this were Aristotle's view, then clearly my position is false.

Ackrill points out that in *De Anima* Aristotle specifies the body actualized by soul as (i) potentially living and (ii) organic (composed of organic parts). But Aristotle tells us elsewhere that a genuine organic part is capable of performing its function, and that requires the presence of soul (*Gen. An.* II.1.734b24). But, if soul is present in the parts that compose an organic body, then the body (the matter) is always actually alive and not always potentially alive (as I claim).

There is good evidence, however, that the parts of the body are not alive in the same way that the composite itself is; in fact they are only potentially alive: (1) Aristotle calls the parts of animals "potentialities"—"Evidently even of the things that are thought to be substances, most are only potentialities— e.g., the parts of animals (for none of them exists separately; and when they are separated, then they too exist only as matter) . . . for none of them is one but they are like a heap before it is fused by heat and some one thing is made of the bits" (*Metaph.* VII.16.1040b5–9). (2) Aristotle thinks that one cannot define the part of an animal by stating its function or capacity without reference to the whole animal—"for the semicircle is defined by the circle; and so is the finger by the whole body, for a finger is such and such part of a man" (*Metaph.* VII.10.1036a9–11).

Two things are true of the organic parts of animals for Aristotle: (i) they must be defined in terms of their function (in Ackrill's terms, as possessing certain powers); (ii) they must be defined as possessing those powers *potentially*, because they have the capacities or powers only as parts of the actual, living animal. The two points are not contradictory if we bear in mind that there are degrees of potentiality and actuality. A part of an animal, a finger, is only potentially capable of functioning in the sense that it is not capable of functioning in itself, or separately, but only as a part of an organized whole, an actually existing human being. So, the organic parts of an animal (the matter of the composite) are only potentially alive in the sense that they are not *in themselves* alive. They do have in themselves, however, a capacity or power to be alive—a capacity for a capacity.

But we must make distinctions concerning potentiality and actuality; for the moment we are speaking of them in an unqualified way. We can speak of something as a knower either as
when we say that man is a knower, meaning that man falls
within the class of beings that know or have knowledge, or as
when we are speaking of a man who possesses a knowledge of
grammar. (Each of these is potential, but not in the same way,
the one being a potential knower, because his kind or matter is
such and such, the other because when he wants to he can
contemplate, if nothing external prevents him.) [417a22–28]

The potential knower in the first sense has the capacity for a
capacity. A human being, because he or she *is* a human being,
has a capacity to have knowledge of various sorts. For Aristotle,
the possession of knowledge of various sorts is also a capacity,
or potentiality, in relation to its exercise. Indeed, having knowledge (versus exercising knowledge) is a classic example of CE
potentiality and actuality. A knower has the potentiality to have
knowledge, Aristotle tells us, because "his kind or matter is of
a certain sort." So, the capacity for the capacity—which is having, but not exercising, knowledge—is retained by the knower
so long as he or she is a human being. In the kind of case in
which I am interested, the sort of potentiality associated with
matter in a composite substance (a capacity for the capacity to
live a human life) is retained so long as the matter is of the
appropriate sort. The matter cannot be of any kind; it must be
potentially alive and human.

The difference between the level of potentiality and actuality
that I have labeled *capacity and exercise* and the level that I have
said applies to matter and form in the composite should be
fairly clear. Where does PE potentiality and actuality fit into
my schema? This kind of potentiality differs from both the
capacity for the capacity to know (i.e., the level of potentiality
I have associated with the matter of a composite substance)
and the capacity to know versus the exercise of knowledge
(i.e., CE potentiality and actuality). If we think about the acquisition of knowledge as a process of development directed
toward an end, PE potentiality and actuality can be fitted into
the picture. According to this use of the potentiality/actuality

distinction, when one says someone is a potential knower, one means he or she is en route toward acquiring those capacities which constitute being a knower. He or she has learned grammar and geometry, for example, but not astronomy and philosophy. The two levels of capacity differ (hence the two levels of potentiality differ) in that a person who has a capacity to acquire knowledge, but has not yet begun to do so, cannot truly be said to know anything; whereas the person who has acquired some knowledge, but has not developed the capacity to know fully, can truly be said to know something. Let us apply this distinction between two levels of potentiality to a composite substance, a human being. In its material aspect, in its way of being as potentiality, this composite is always potentially human. Viewed as a being that is en route toward its end (the full realization of its form or essence), our composite is also potentially human, but in a different sense. In this way of being, according to this sense of potentiality, the composite is potentially human in the sense that it has not yet fully realized its nature.

In the case of form and matter in the composite substance, as in the other examples of actuality and potentiality, actual being determines potential being. As before, the determination is of two basic sorts—actuality is prior in being and in definition to potentiality. Actuality or form is prior in being to potentiality or matter because the matter exists toward the end or form. In discussing the priority in being of the actual over the potential, Aristotle says that "matter exists in a potential state, just because it may attain to its form; and when it exists actually, then it is in its form" (*Metaph.* IX.8.1050a15–16; also 1088b1, 1092a3–5).

Further, actuality is prior to potentiality in definition because the matter of a composite substance is defined, insofar as it has a definition, by reference to a corresponding actuality. This claim provokes a couple of questions: Why does Aristotle think that we can define matter only in relation to form? Why can we not define it quite independently of form, in terms of its own material qualities? The answer is that Aristotle thinks (i) that a definition should tell you what something is and (ii) that matter exists or is toward or for the sake of form. And so it should be defined as potentially enformed. In talking about various approaches to definition, Aristotle says: "And so, in definition, those who define a house as stones, bricks, and timbers are speaking of the potential house, for these are the matter" (1043a14–16). The description of the matter as the "potential house" reveals the way that Aristotle thinks reality is ordered. It is directional. In this case, that means that matter, potentiality as matter, is toward form just as the composite substances themselves are directional. They exist toward the full realization of their forms. In both cases, the teleological character of the structure of being has a similar consequence for definitions, for in both cases the definition of the potentiality must be given in terms of the corresponding actuality.

I now return to the issue of the unity of form and matter in the composite substance. Clearly, Aristotle thinks that viewing matter and form as potentiality and actuality solves the problem of their unity, but it is not yet clear why he thinks this. Aristotle states his conviction in a context in which he is discussing the problem of the unity of the object of definition. My discussion of the definitional dependency of potential being on actual being is certainly relevant to the problem of unity, for it explained that matter and form are not two definitionally independent beings. Because what it is to be a potentiality is dependent upon what an actuality is, composite substances are unified objects of definition. Matter is definitionally dependent upon form. There is, therefore, one definition: matter and form, as ways of being of the composite substance, satisfy that definition to different degrees.

In order to grasp the kind of unity that composite substances have according to my account of the relationship between matter and form, we can contrast it with the kind of unity they have according to another interpretation: namely, the view, which I addressed earlier, that forms are accidental properties of matter. Accidental unities are "bundles" of two or more beings joined together by the predication relationship. I said earlier that there is good reason to think that Aristotle would not find this kind of unity adequate for substances. And, indeed, in his account of the unity of the composite substance, Aristotle warns against explanations of this type, which join together two beings by some relationship or other (VIII.6.1045b7–19). In contrast, if matter and form are understood as potentiality and actuality—as two ways of being the substance, rather than two beings—then composite substances are not "bundles" as accidental beings are. The two ways of being are "internally" linked, in that what it is to be potential being is determined by what actual being is. The definition of potentiality is determined by the corresponding actuality. By holding that matter should be viewed as potentiality, and form as actuality, Aristotle is taking a radical step in denying independent definitions to matter. On the other hand, by doing so, he provides a solution to the unity problem—in particular, a solution that shows how composite substances are unified and have one definition.

Let us return for a moment to the issue of whether or not it is correct to think of an Aristotelian form as a property of the matter in the composite substance. Earlier, I argued against this view on the grounds that there is good reason to think that Aristotle would not allow that form is either an accidental or a necessary property of matter. And I urged that we try to understand the relationship between form and matter by using the notions of potentiality and actuality. But, one might argue, the view that the matter is the potential substance and the form is the actual substance is compatible with the view that form is a property of the matter. According to my interpretation of what Aristotle means by saying that the matter is potentially the substance and the form is actually the substance, however, the two views are not compatible. For I have said that the matter of a composite substance is always potentially F (where "F" is shorthand for the essence of the substance in question). But, if its form or essence were a property of the matter of the substance, then it would follow that the matter *is* F and not always *potentially* F. So, if my interpretation of Aristotle's doctrine that matter is potentiality and form is actuality is correct, then the form or essence is not a property of the matter.[21]

----

[21]In order to argue persuasively that form is a property of matter for Aristotle, it is necessary to do more than defeat my analysis of potentiality (matter) and

In the next chapter, I address a basic issue for the understanding of Aristotle's essentialism: namely, the ontological status of form or essence. For the line of argument in the present chapter might lead one to wonder how to think of form or essence. If they are neither properties of the composite nor properties of matter, what are they? We can make some headway with this issue by considering Aristotle's reflections concerning whether the principles and causes of substances are universal or individual. This famous *aporia*, described by Aristotle as "the most difficult of all" is the subject of the next chapter.

---

actuality (form). For the first argument I gave against the "form is a property of matter" view—namely, that the resulting composite substance would merely be an accidental unity—is entirely independent of the details of my interpretation of potentiality and actuality.

Chapter 5

THE ONTOLOGICAL STATUS
OF ESSENCE

In the preceding chapter, I argued that an Aristotelian form or essence is not a property; in particular, I argued that it is neither a property of the composite substance nor a property of the matter of a composite substance. This negative conclusion, I remarked, leaves us with no clear idea of what an essence might be if it is not some kind of property of the substance. I explained that Aristotle thought that its form or essence is the cause of being of an individual, composite substance; its essence is responsible for there being an actual, determinate, unified substance rather than a heap of matter, potential and indeterminate. From this discussion, we know something about what composite substances are like and something about what their matter is like, but very little about what their form or essence is like beyond its causal role. In the present chapter, I provide a positive characterization of form or essence by explaining that, for Aristotle, form or essence is an individual and not a universal. Indeed, the intent of this chapter is to replace the traditional interpretation of Aristotelian essences—that an essence is a cluster of universal properties— with an interpretation according to which an essence is an individual substance, though not, of course, a composite or sensible substance.[1]

[1] I am not the first to suggest that Aristotle's essences are individual rather

According to the traditional interpretation of Aristotle, the forms or essences of composite substances should be thought of as *species-forms*: i.e., forms or essences that are common to all members of a natural kind or species. All human beings, for example, share the same species-form or species-essence. On this view, forms or essences are universal in the sense that there is shared human essence. And this common human essence is constituted by a set of essential properties (whatever they might turn out to be). Of course, one could also hold that, in addition to these shared, or universal, essential properties (which together constitute the species-form or species-essence), there are also individual essential properties that are unique to an individual subject, that are part of *its* essence—but not part of any other individual's essence, not even an individual of the same kind or species. These individual, essential properties are not a part of the traditional interpretation of Aristotelian essentialism, however, and so we can postpone discussion of them till the next chapter, which compares Aristotle's essentialism with Kripke's.

For the present, I want to strengthen my case for a different characterization of essences from the traditional one: instead of characterizing essences as properties and as universals, I

than species-essences. The view was originally discussed in a pair of papers by Wilfrid Sellars and Rogers Albritton ("Substance and Form in Aristotle," *Journal of Philosophy*, 22 [Oct. 1957], 698–708). Albritton's paper is particularly useful in marshaling the texts and philosophical difficulties that face the individual essences interpretation. More recently, Michael Frede ("Substance in Aristotle's Metaphysics," *Aristotle on Nature and Living Things*, ed. Allan Gotthelf [Pittsburgh: Mathesis Publications, 1985], 17–26) presents a particular forms interpretation that is similar to mine in several respects. The basic difference concerns the function assigned to forms or essences. According to Frede, individual forms function as principles of identity for objects; its form is that aspect of an object that must remain the same over time and through change. Edwin Hartman ("Aristotle on the Identity of Substance and Essence," *Philosophical Review*, 85 [Oct. 1976], 545–561) adopts an individual essence view, and also explains the function of individual essences in terms of the problem of the identity of substances over time. My interpretation differs from both Frede's and Hartman's with respect to the issue of the function of Aristotle's individual essences. I believe there is very little evidence for the Frede-Hartman proposal that the issue is substantial identity. Rather, the essence is the cause of being of a substance; the central function of essence is to explain the actual existence of a unified substance.

argue that they are substances and particulars, or individuals. I have already made a case against the idea that Aristotelian essences are the properties of substances. In the course of showing that they are not universals, but rather individuals, the case against viewing them as the properties of substances will be strengthened. For what the traditional view means when it characterizes essences as properties of substances is that essences are universals, those properties which the substance shares with other members of its kind. So, even though an argument which shows that forms or essences are not universal does not at the same time establish that they are not properties of the substance (they could be individual properties of it), nonetheless it does remove one basic motivation from the traditional view for holding they are properties. In this way, the discussion of the present chapter will support the claim from the preceding chapter that forms or essences are not properties of the substance. Further, the idea that forms or essences are individuals and substances provides us with an alternative to the traditional interpretation of them as universal properties associated with natural kinds or species.

In *Metaphysics* III.6, Aristotle formulates the question of whether forms or essences are universal or individual as an *aporia* concerning how to think of the principles of substances:[2]

> We must not only raise these questions about the principles, but also ask whether they are universals or what we call particulars. If they are universal, they will not be substances; for nothing common indicates a "this" but rather a "such," but substance is a "this." But, if we can set up the common predicate as a "this," then Socrates will be many animals—himself and man and animal, if each of these indicates a "this" and a unity. If, then, the principles are universal, these things follow. If, on the other hand, they are not universals but like particulars, they

<hr />

[2]This *aporia* is also stated in XI.2.1060b20–24 and XIII.10.1086b20–7a35. I believe that Alan Code is correct in pointing out that some of the discussion in *Metaphysics* VII can be profitably read as a working-out of this *aporia*. ("The Aporematic Approach to Primary Being in *Metaphysics* Z," *Canadian Journal of Philosophy*, supp. vol. 10 [1984], 1–20. Although Code and I do not reach the same conclusion about the solution of the *aporia*, my thinking has been influenced and helped by his paper.

will not be knowable. For knowledge of anything is universal. Therefore, if there is to be knowledge of the principles, there will be other principles prior to them, which are predicated universally of them. [1003a5–17]

What does Aristotle mean by the terms "universal" and "particular" in this passage? According to Aristotle, a universal (e.g., man) is by nature predicated of many things, whereas a particular (Callias) is not. Earlier, in Chapter 2, I said that Aristotelian universals are always instantiated; they do not exist independently of some object or other. We can now add to this picture of Aristotelian universals the characteristic that they are predicated of a plurality of subjects (i.e., more than one subject).[3] So, according to Aristotle's definitions of the terms "universal" and "particular," the question raised in this text is whether form or essence is universal and predicated of many things, or whether form or essence is particular, like an individual composite substance. In this passage, Aristotle also describes the opposition in question by means of terms I have here translated as "this" and "such."[4] The contrast between a "this," or individual, and a "such," or universal, is that the former are separate beings (i.e., ontologically basic). This can be seen from two of Aristotle's remarks. First, he tells us that substances are "thisses" and that universals are "suches." And we know from Chapter 2 that he thinks substances are ontologically basic and universals are not. Substances do not exist in another being as their subject, whereas universals exist only insofar as they exist in a subject. It is in connection with this idea that Aristotle's explanation of what it would mean to say that a universal is a "this," or an individual, makes sense. For he says that if universals were "thisses," then an individual substance would be many substances (e.g., Socrates would be many animals). We could no longer think of the universals as existing in a subject, a substance; rather, they should be

[3]This definition of universal and particular is given in *De Interpretatione* 17a38–b1; in *Metaphysics* III, the definitions are similar except that "particular" is equated with "one in number" (999b34–1000a).

[4]The Greek terms are "τόδε τι" which I translate as "this" and "τοιόνδε" which I translate as "such."

thought of as independently existing substances. What seemed to be an individual substance, Socrates, turns out to be many substances if universals themselves are individual substances, or "thisses."

The *aporia* is generated by two deep philosophical intuitions that Aristotle inherited from earlier philosophers, especially Plato, and that he himself endorsed.[5] The first intuition is that the universal is the object of knowledge and definition. The other is that substances are separate (ontologically basic) individual beings. At first glance, these two positions do not conflict; indeed, it is difficult to see how an *aporia* can be generated from them. Instead, they appear to suggest that individual composite substances are known through their universal forms or essences. That is to say, the two intuitions appear to support the traditional interpretation of Aristotelian essentialism, according to which essences of composite substances are species-essences. On further reflection, however, the fact that Aristotle believes that his views generate an *aporia* might lead us to question the traditional interpretation, precisely because it does not provide us with the raw material from which to construct an *aporia*.

In order to appreciate Aristotle's difficulty, it is crucial to understand that his question concerns the ontological character of the *principles* of substances: namely, the ontological character of forms or essences. From this perspective, the claim that all knowledge and definition is of the universal supports the characterization of forms and essences as universal. But the claim that substance is separate and individual supports the characterization of forms and essences as separate and individual. The latter point rests on a further claim, that forms or essences (the principles of composite substances) are themselves substances; they are not, of course, composite substances, but are substances nonetheless. There is ample evidence in the central books of the *Metaphysics* that Aristotle considers form or es-

---

[5]Aristotle gives Socrates the credit for turning philosophy toward ethical issues by seeking the universal and originating the pursuit of definitions (*Metaphysics* 987b1–4, 1086b2–5). He commends Plato for conceiving of the forms as separate beings (*Metaphysics* 1040b27–28).

sence to be substance;[6] indeed, there is even persuasive evidence that he considers form or essence, rather than the composite substance, to be *primary* substance.[7] These are the contours of Aristotle's *aporia* concerning form or essence, and perhaps it is already clear why he calls it "the most difficult of all" (1087a13).

One wing of the *aporia* is based primarily on epistemological considerations—the idea that definition and knowledge are of universals. Definition is the answer to the question "What is it?" Aristotle tells us that it was Socrates, seeking the universal in ethics, who first focused attention on definitions (987b1–4, 1086b2–5). If definition is of universals, and if definition is also the statement of the essence, then it seems that essence is universal. Further, if all knowledge is of universals, and if a necessary condition for knowledge of things is knowledge of their essences (1031b7, 20–21), then surely essence must be universal. But, if we are to understand and be persuaded by these skeletal arguments, we need to understand and be convinced that definition (knowledge) is of universals. Aristotle confirms this view, and he presents arguments in favor of it in *Metaphysics* VII; in § 1 of the present chapter, I review his arguments.

The other wing of the *aporia* is based on the notion that universals are not substances. Aristotle means that universals are just not the sort of things that could be substances. But if universals are not substances, and if essence and form are universals, and if essence or form are the principles or causes of sensible substances, then a nonsubstance would be the principle or cause of a substance. From this it would follow that a nonsubstance is prior to a substance, since a principle is prior

---

[6] In Aristotle's discussion of substance in *Metaphysics* v.8, he mentions form or essence three times (1017b14–16, 1017b21–23, 1017b24–26). Essence is mentioned at *Metaphysics* VII.3.1028b34–36, and form is called "substance" throughout that chapter, along with the matter and the composite. Also see *Metaphysics* 1039b20–23.

[7] In the *Metaphysics* (1037a25–30, 1041b25–28), Aristotle gives primacy to form or essence. The idea that form or essence, rather than the composite individual, is primary substance is a departure from the *Categories*, where the composite is given that honor.

to the thing of which it is a principle; but that is impossible, since we know (Chapter 2) that substance is prior to nonsubstance. As I explained, substance is prior to nonsubstance in that substances are the ontologically basic beings; all other beings inhere in them. In particular, universals do not exist independently of substances, and so they could not be prior to substances; nor could they be the principles of substances. In order to understand and accept this argument, however, we need to understand and be convinced that no universal is a substance. Aristotle develops arguments for this claim in *Metaphysics* VII.13, and I shall discuss those arguments in § 2 below.

As I said in Chapter 1, Aristotle thinks that a full appreciation of a philosophical *aporia* (and the possibility of its resolution) depends upon a full exploration of the difficulties attendant upon either of the alternatives. Aristotle's solution of the *aporia* in question consists in a modification of one of its wings: namely, the claim that all knowledge and definition is of the universal. For, in his discussion of the *aporia* in *Metaphysics* XIII.10, Aristotle resolves the dilemma by distinguishing between actual knowledge, which is of the individual, and potential knowledge, which is of the universal. This distinction allows the possibility of knowing individual essences and forms, and thus disarms the basic argument against them.[8] I discuss Aristotle's resolution of the *aporia* in § 3 below.

[8]Against this interpretation, one might want to argue that if it were right, then Aristotle does not really resolve the *aporia*. By embracing one alternative through disarming the basic objections to it, one might argue, Aristotle is not taking the objections seriously enough. One might argue that the resolution should be some third, entirely different way of conceptualizing the issues. If, however, we look at what is very likely Aristotle's model for an *aporia*, and its resolution, we can find a similar strategy of resolution to the one I propose for Aristotle. I refer to Meno's paradox with respect to learning. We know from the *Posterior Analytics* that Aristotle was familiar with this *aporia* (71a28–30). The *aporia* in Plato's *Meno* concerns the very possibility of learning: either one is learning something one already knows or something one does not. But, if the first option, then one does not need to learn it (since one already knows it); and, if the second option, then how could one ever begin to learn about it (since one does not even know what "it" is)? The conclusion of the argument is that all learning is impossible. Now, Socrates resolves this *aporia* much in the same way that I hold Aristotle resolves his *aporia* concerning universal or

I have said that forms or essences are substances, though not composite substances, and I explain in the present chapter that Aristotle thinks of them as individuals and not as universals. One important issue raised by these claims is how to understand the idea of an "individual" applied to forms or essences. What does it mean to say that forms or essences are individuals? Aristotle cites an individual composite substance (Callias) as an example of a particular, but there are surely important differences between composite substances such as Callias and forms or essences such as Callias' soul. What does it mean to say that Callias' soul is an individual or a particular? I discuss this issue in § 4 below.

1. The Universal Is the Object of Definition and Knowledge

We can begin to understand the claim of the universal to be the object of definition and knowledge by distinguishing several reasons that Aristotle gives for this position. Later, it will be necessary to consider the case of definition separately, for Aristotle treats that topic at some length in the central books of the *Metaphysics*.

Aristotle frequently makes a contrast between the objects of knowledge and the objects of perception: universals are the object of knowledge, and particulars are the objects of perception.[9] There seem to be two kinds of reasons that Aristotle gives for this position—one concerning the impossibility of knowing an unlimited number of individuals, the other concerning the impossibility of knowing material individuals.

What is the difficulty in connection with knowledge of an unlimited number of particulars? And what role does the universal play in relation to this difficulty? In the *Metaphysics*, Aristotle explains in the following terms:

---

individual principles: namely, by accepting with modifications one wing of the dilemma. For Socrates argues that we do indeed (in a sense) already know what we are learning; his resolution is the doctrine of recollection.

[9] Aristotle pairs perception with individuals and knowledge with universals (*An. Post.* 81a38–b9, 87b29–34; *Metaphysics* 999a24–b3).

If, on the one hand, there is nothing apart from particulars, and the particulars are unlimited, how is it possible to obtain knowledge of the unlimited particulars? For all things that we know, we know insofar as they have some unity and identity, and insofar as some attribute belongs to them universally. [999a26–29]

A universal attribute or property, that which is shared by a number of particulars, provides a basis of unity and sameness for an unlimited number of particulars. We can know an indefinite number of particulars through the grasp of a single universal. In contrast, perception brings before us a mere particular. The universal is an epistemic principle of unity, in that it is responsible for our being able to know an unlimited number of particulars.

The second basic consideration that Aristotle adduces in support of his claim that knowledge is of the universal, and that perception is of the particular, concerns our apprehension of material particulars. Here the universal is viewed primarily as a stable object for knowledge—in contrast to material individuals, which pass in and out of existence. Material individuals, because they are transient, are the objects of perception, whereas universals, because they are permanent, are the objects of knowledge:

For this reason, also, there is neither definition nor demonstration of sensible individual substances, because they have matter whose nature is such that they are capable both of being and not being; for which reason all the individual instances of them are destructible. If, then, demonstration is of necessary truths and definition involves knowledge, and if, just as knowledge cannot be sometimes knowledge and sometimes ignorance, but the state that varies thus is opinion, so too demonstration and definition cannot vary thus, but it is opinion that deals with that which can be other than it is; clearly there can be neither definition nor demonstration of sensible individuals. [1039b27–40a2]

There is no definition or demonstrative knowledge concerning individual composite substances because these are transient beings owing to their material aspect. Material particulars are not stable objects for definition and knowledge. Another reason Aristotle gives for holding that composite substances are not objects of definition and knowledge also concerns their material aspect, for he holds that matter is "indefinite" (1037a24–30) and "unknowable" (1036a9). But if the material aspect of the composite is indefinite and unknowable, then it is hard to see how the composite itself could be a satisfactory object of knowledge and definition.

It is useful to pause at this point and summarize the considerations that apparently lead Aristotle to hold that all knowledge (definition) is of universals and not of particulars. Only the universal can provide us with an epistemic principle of unity and sameness that unites an unlimited number of particulars. The particulars are unlimited in the sense that there is no limit to the number of them that could exist. The universal provides an epistemic principle of unity, in that it provides a means of knowing an unlimited number of particulars through knowing a universal property of them. Further, material particulars are not appropriate objects of knowledge. First of all, knowledge is stable; it does not change as time passes. But material particulars, because they are *material* particulars, pass in and out of existence. Not only that, but their material aspect also means that they are to some degree "indeterminate" and to some degree "unknowable." In sum, the objects of knowledge should provide an epistemic principle of unity, they should be stable, and they should be fully knowable. Material particulars such as composite substances seem to fail on all three counts; universals, on the other hand, appear to satisfy all three criteria. On the basis of these considerations, then, we might conclude that Aristotle has good reason to hold that all knowledge and definition are of the universal.

In *Metaphysics* VII.15, Aristotle offers an additional argument against the possibility of defining particulars or individuals. Here the issue is not whether an individual could be a stable object of definition, for Aristotle considers the case of an *eternal* individual. The problem stems from the nature of definition itself, rather than from some inadequacy with regard to the proposed object of definition. Assume an eternal, unique individual such as the sun. Any definition of it (i.e., any list of distinguishing attributes) is only contingently a unique definition of it: "if another thing with the stated attributes comes into existence, clearly it will be a sun; the definition therefore is common" (1040a33–35). In other words, definitions are stated in words that have, either actually or potentially, application to more than one particular object. For example, the Aristotelian definition of soul as "the first actuality of a body having life potentially" is a definition that applies to all souls. The definition is a definition not of any particular soul, but of many souls. It is universal. Here, the reason that definition is of the universal rather than of the particular is a consequence of what a definition is, not a consequence of some flaw in the proposed object of definition.

These Aristotelian reflections concerning knowledge and definition pose an obvious problem for the line of interpretation I developed in Chapter 4. For there I claimed that substances, (i.e., composite substances) had definitions and essences in a privileged sense, and I said that this was so because substances are highly unified beings. But now there appears to be a tension between (i) the idea that composite substances, *qua* substances, have definitions and essences in a privileged sense and (ii) the idea that, as particular and material, they are not the objects of knowledge and definition at all. This is even more problematic if we recall that definitions are statements of essence for Aristotle. For if we push the line of thought to its limit, it begins to appear that individual, material substances do not have definitions and, hence, do not have essences at all.

Part of the tension in these positions is eased by Aristotle's explanations of in what sense and for what reason the individual composite substance does not have a definition. Aristotle's position is that the composite substance as a whole is not the object of definition. Rather, its definition is of its form or essence:

> And we have stated that in the definition of the substance the material parts will not be present. For they are not even parts of the substance in that sense, but of the concrete substance, but of this there is in a sense a definition, and in a sense there is not; for there is no definition of it with its matter, for this is

indefinite, but there is a definition of it with reference to its primary substance—e.g., in the case of man, the definition of soul—for the substance is the indwelling form, from which and the matter, the so-called concrete substance, is derived. [1037a24–30]

So, the idea that a composite substance, as material, lacks a definition is only a partial statement of Aristotle's view. For he holds that they do indeed have definitions: namely, the definitions of their form or essence.[10] This position is exactly what we would expect, given Aristotle's analysis of the composite in terms of potentiality and actuality. As we saw in Chapter 4, Aristotle holds that the definition of the composite substance is given in terms of its form or actuality, and not in terms of its matter or potentiality. Thus, the claim that material individuals, because of their matter, cannot be the objects of knowledge and definition does not rule out composite substances as objects of knowledge and definition; for they are known through their forms or essences. Further, once this point is seen, the argument concerning the unsuitability of material individuals as epistemic objects no longer has any relevance to the question concerning whether form or essence is universal or particular.

It is very different, however, with the two other considerations in favor of universal forms or essences. For it is difficult to see how any particular could function as an epistemic principle of unity in the way that Aristotle says the universal functions. And it is equally difficult to see how definition could be of particulars, given Aristotle's idea that definitions are inherently applicable to more than one entity, i.e., that definitions are inherently of universals.

One way to accommodate these characteristics of knowledge

---

[10]This point bears on Aristotle's reflections concerning which things are identical to their essences. The issue is discussed at some length in *Metaphysics* VII.6 and is brought up again in VIII.3. In the latter text, Aristotle says that soul and the essence of soul are the same, but man and the essence of man are not, unless one is using "man" to mean "soul of man." The essence of man is stated in the definition of "soul," so if one uses "man" to refer to the composite, then man is not identical to its essence (1043a29–b4, 1037b4–7).

and definition and their objects is to hold that the universal is the principle or origin of knowledge—and hence prior to the individual in the epistemic realm—but that the individual is prior to the universal in the realm of being, or ontologically. Indeed, in one of his statements of the *aporia*, Aristotle mentions this possibility: "Therefore, if there is to be knowledge of the principles, there must be other principles prior to them, which are universally predicated of them" (1003a14–15). The difficulty with this compromise is that that universal epistemological principles would be prior to the individual principles. As we shall see in § 2 below, however, Aristotle does not think that any universal could be substance. But, if universals are nonsubstances, then a nonsubstance (the universal epistemological principle) would be prior to a substance—a view Aristotle rejects (*Metaphysics* XIII.10.1086b37–1087a1). Moreover, as we shall see in § 3 below, Aristotle does not develop the position that the individual is ontologically prior to the universal, but the universal is epistemologically prior to the individual. Instead, he claims that the individual is epistemologically prior to the universal. Why does Aristotle hold that no universal is substance?

2. No Universal Is Substance

The universal is one of four candidates for being substance that Aristotle lists early in *Metaphysics* VII, and in chapter 13 he discusses at some length the possibility that the universal is substance. Although the arguments in VII.13 are compressed and difficult, the conclusion is stated at the outset: "The universal also is thought by some to be in the fullest sense a cause, and a principle; therefore, let us attack the discussion of this point, also. For it seems impossible that anything said universally is substance" (1038b6–9). In this section, I explain the kinds of considerations that Aristotle gives in support of this conclusion.[11] Before doing so, however, let us turn to another

---

[11]Scholars have employed two strategies to avoid taking Aristotle's conclusion at its face value. First, since it is clear that many of the points Aristotle

feature of Aristotle's approach to essences and universals that
deserves comment.

Metaphysics VII.13 opens with a summary of the progress of
Aristotle's investigation into substance:

> Let us again return to the subject of our inquiry, which is sub-
> stance. As the subject and the essence and the compound of
> these are called substance, so too is the universal. About two
> of these we have spoken; about the essence and the sub-
> strate. . . . The universal is also thought by some to be in the
> fullest sense a cause, and a principle; therefore, let us attack the
> discussion of this point, also. [1038b1–8]

What is very striking about this text, in relation to the traditional interpretation of Aristotle's essentialism, is the fact that
Aristotle treats essences and universals independently. Not
only, then, is Aristotle's conclusion that universals are not substances (in a context where that position has the clear implication that essences are not universal) at odds with the
traditional interpretation, but Aristotle's basic way of thinking
about essences and universals reveals a striking divergence
between his approach and the traditional interpretation of his
essentialism. For Aristotle asks the two questions—whether
the essence is substance and whether the universal is substance—independently, which casts doubt on a fundamental
connection between essence and universal in his thought. That
is to say, the very fact that Aristotle treats the two topics separately, quite apart from his conclusions, casts doubt on the
species-form or species-essence interpretation; for that view

---

makes in chapters 13 and 14 are directed against a Platonic theory of Forms
and definitions, it is possible to read these chapters in a restricted way—as a
criticism of Platonic Forms as substances, rather than as a criticism of universals. Or, alternatively, one can argue, as Michael Woods does in "Problems
in *Metaphysics* Z, Chapter 13" (in *Aristotle: A Collection of Critical Essays*, ed.
J. M. E. Moravcsik [New York: Doubleday, 1967], pp. 215–238), that the arguments apply only to some universals—i.e., those above the species level.
Neither of these strategies is successful. Although it is clear that Aristotle is
concerned with Platonic Forms in these chapters, and although it is also clear
that in this connection he argues against taking higher universals as the substances of things, it is equally clear that some of his arguments have a more
general application. They apply to all Aristotelian universals.

assumes a basic conceptual connection between essence and universal that is strikingly absent from the discussion we are considering.

Why does Aristotle think that nothing predicated universally, or no universal, is substance? He gives three basic reasons in *Metaphysics* VII.13. First, he constructs an argument that turns on the idea that the substance of something is peculiar to it and not common or shared. A second argument turns on the idea that substance is a subject and is not predicated of a subject. Earlier (Chapter 2) I explained that Aristotle sometimes described this feature of substance by saying that substances are "separate." Finally, he explains that substance is a "this" and contrasts substance with the universal, which is a "such." Before examining these considerations in more detail, we need to recall Aristotle's definition of a universal: a universal is (by nature) said or predicated of many things. Each of the arguments I discuss hinges on this conception of a universal.

The first consideration is that an entity's substance is unique to it, rather than shared with other entities. Aristotle incorporates this idea in an argument (1038b9–15) that constructs a dilemma for someone who would think of the substance of a thing (i.e., its essence) as a universal that is by nature shared.[12] Aristotle reasons:

(1) The substance of each thing is that which is peculiar to it, that which does not belong to anything else.

(2) The universal is common because what is called universal is such as to belong to more than one thing.

Now suppose, given premises (1) and (2), that a universal is a substance. We can ask, "of which of the things that it belongs to is it the substance?" There are two possibilities:

(3) Either it is the substance of all of them or of none of them.

Aristotle next argues against the first disjunct, since the second is just the conclusion that the universal is not a substance:

[12]My understanding of this argument is indebted to Alan Code, "No Universal Is a Substance," *Paideia: Special Aristotle Issue* (1978), 65–74.

(4) It cannot be the substance of all of them.

Suppose that the universal *is* the substance of one of its instances. Then that instance will be each of the others, as well:

(5) If it is the substance of one, then this one will be the others, also;

for

(6) Things whose substance is one and whose essence is one are themselves also one.

In order for (6) to provide support for (5), it must be understood as claiming that two things with a numerically identical substance or essence are themselves one. My explanation of the claim in (6) assumes that here Aristotle equates the substance of a thing with its essence, an assumption that is supported by the fact that Aristotle quite frequently describes form or essence as substance in a context where it is clear that he means the substance of a composite substance.[13] Understood in this way premise (6) elaborates upon what Aristotle means in premise (1) when he says that the substance of each thing is peculiar to it.[14] But if the instances are all identical, then the substance in question is no longer universal, given the definition of universal in premise (1). For there is no longer a number of things of which it is predicated. And, given premise (3), if the universal is not the substance of all of its instances, then it is not the substance of any of them.

This ingenious argument tries to show that if we understand the substance of a thing to be that which unifies it, and if we understand that a universal is predicated of many things, then we will see that a universal cannot be the substance of a thing. If it were, then it would no longer be a universal, for there would no longer be many things of which it is predicated. Just

---

[13]See the texts mentioned in note 6 above.

[14]In *Metaphysics* VII.16, Aristotle says: "In general, nothing common is substance; for substance does not belong to any thing but to itself and to that which has it, of which it is the substance" (1040b23–25).

as we saw Aristotle arguing (§ 1 above) that, given what a definition is, it is always of the universal, here we see him arguing that given what a universal is, and given what the substance of something is, nothing universal can be the substance of something.

The argument turns on two points. The first is Aristotle's definition of a universal; the second is contained in (6) above, the idea that things whose essence and substance are one are themselves one. The second idea should remind us of Aristotle's characterization of form or essence as the cause of being of a substance, where one aspect of that role is that form or essence causes the matter to constitute an actual, unified individual, rather than a heap. Here we see an elaboration of the unifying role that Aristotle assigns to form or essence, in that he makes it clear that a common or shared essence would transform many things into one thing because essences are principles of unity. Earlier, in the preceding chapter, I had explained the unifying function as operating on the material parts of a composite substance. But, as this argument makes clear, Aristotle also thinks that the unifying function of essence could also operate on individuals; a shared universal essence would make many individuals into one.

The second argument (1038b15–16) against the possibility of universal substances also turns on Aristotle's definition of the universal:

(1) Substance is said to be that which is not predicated of a subject.

(2) The universal is always said to be predicated of some subject.

Therefore,

(3) The universal is not substance.

In this argument, Aristotle emphasizes a feature of substances that has been important right from the beginning of book VII: namely, that substances are the ontologically basic beings, the subjects. A universal, by definition, is not a basic being because it is always predicated of a subject. Since this is just what a universal is, no universal can be a substance.

It is interesting in connection with this argument to recall the discussion in § 5 of Chapter 4. For it might be objected that, according to this argument, form or essence itself would turn out not to be substance. As pointed out in Chapter 4, Aristotle sometimes says that form has matter as its subject. In my discussion of the relationship between form and matter, however, I emphasized that it would be a mistake to think of that relationship as equivalent to the relationship between a property or universal and an individual subject. But if Aristotle does not think of the two relationships as similar in logical structure, then this argument does not imply that form and essence are not substance. On the other hand, given that form and essence are substance, then the argument does count against thinking of them as universal.

It is important to stress one feature of Aristotle's definition of the universal, which might not be entirely clear yet. Earlier, in Chapter 2, I said that Aristotle did not think that universals existed separately from their instances. His definition of the universal can be seen to reflect this view. In saying that universals *by nature* are such as to be predicated of many things, Aristotle means that they do not exist in separation from the many things of which they are predicated: "Further, that which is one cannot be in many places at the same time, but that which is common is present in many places at the same time; so that clearly no universal exists separately from the particulars" (1040b25–27). In this passage, Aristotle proceeds to say of the Platonists that they were right to say that their Forms exist separately, if they thought of their Forms as substances, but wrong to conceive of form as one over many. Presumably, the Platonists' mistake was to hold that their substances—the Forms—are both separate *and* universal (i.e., one over many). As substances, Aristotle thinks, Platonic Forms would have to be separate; but if they are, then they cannot also be characterized as universal. In the argument we have been considering, Aristotle makes the same point with respect to his own views. Since Aristotelian substance is separate (i.e., is not said of a subject), it cannot at the same time be universal, since a universal is by definition said of many subjects.

In the context of describing substances as "thisses" and universals as "suches," Aristotle makes a third point about the incompatibility of being a substance versus being a universal (1038b24–1039a3). In this chapter, Aristotle refers to a substance as a "this"; a "such" is used to refer to either a universal or an attribute such as a quality, whether particular or universal. In either use, the entity labeled a "such" is an entity that has a substance as an ontological subject; for, as I explained in Chapter 2, Aristotle holds that attributes and universals alike (i) have substances as their subjects and (ii) do not exist independently of substance.

Let us consider each of these classifications in turn, beginning with universals. In my discussion of Aristotle's description of the *aporia* concerning the principles of substances, I have already mentioned one difficulty that Aristotle expresses in this terminology: namely, the idea that if universals were "thisses" rather than "suches," then a substance would be many substances. If each universal associated with Socrates' definition as a human being were itself a "this," then Socrates would be many individuals (1038b29–34). If, on the other hand, we think of the principle of a substance as consisting of "suches," where the term refers to nonsubstantial beings generally (i.e., whether universal or particular), there is a different unpalatable consequence: namely, that a nonsubstance will be prior to a substance:

> And further it is impossible and absurd that the "this," i.e., the substance, if it consists of parts should not consist of substances nor of what is a "this," but of quality; for that which is not substance, i.e., the quality, will then be prior to substance and to the "this." Which is impossible; for neither in definition nor in time nor in generation can the affections be prior to the substance. [1038b23–28]

As this text makes very clear, Aristotle's basic concern in this chapter is how we should think of the principles of individual composite substances. Given that they are "thisses," he explains why their principles cannot be "suches," where that term refers both to universals generally and to attributes. So, if we apply Aristotle's reasoning to the topic of essence, viewed as a principle or cause of substance, the result is that we ought not to think of form or essence as universal. In this way, Aristotle's dictum that nothing universal is substance must be understood not simply as applying to individual composite substances, but as applying also to form or essence. Once we consider Aristotle's line of reasoning in this chapter, it is very clear that the traditional view—which holds that composite substances are individual, and their forms or essences are universal—does not really get to the heart of Aristotle's dilemma concerning the nature of the principles of substances.

The arguments we have been considering are to the effect that no universal is substance. But the wing of the *aporia* with which we are concerned holds that the principles or causes of substances are not universal. Surely it is possible for the principles of substances to be universal, but for substances to be individual. For example, as the traditional interpretation holds, Socrates is a substance and a particular; his soul, his form or essence, is universal. As I explained earlier in the present chapter, this possibility is ruled out explicitly in Aristotle's discussion of the *aporia*, on the grounds that it would make a nonsubstance the principle of a substance (1086b37–1087a4). And this possibility, in turn, would mean that a nonsubstance is prior to a substance—precisely the reverse of what Aristotle considers the correct relation to be.

In the preceding two sections, I have described the heart of Aristotle's dilemma concerning how to think of the principles of substances. For our purposes, the *aporia* in question concerns how we ought to think of form or essence. There are very good reasons, primarily epistemological, for thinking of form or essence as universal. And there are very good reasons, primarily ontological, for thinking of form or essence as particular. What is Aristotle's solution to this *aporia*?

3. The Resolution of the *Aporia*

In his discussion of the *aporia* in *Metaphysics* xiii.10, Aristotle proposes a resolution that turns upon distinguishing two types of knowledge: actual knowledge, which is of the individual, and potential knowledge, which is of the universal (1087a10–21). The puzzle concerning the principles of substances is that, as we have just seen in §§ 1 and 2, there are good reasons for holding that they are universal and not particular, and also good reasons for holding that they are particular and not universal. The principles must be universal in order that they be knowable, for all knowledge (definition) is of the universal. They must also be particular: if they were universal, then a nonsubstance (i.e., the universal) would be the principle of a substance and prior to a substance. In proposing that there are two types of knowledge, Aristotle denies that all knowledge is of the universal and, in so doing, removes the chief objection facing particular principles and causes. Since Aristotle's resolution of the *aporia* involves the claim that particular principles can be known, the obvious conclusion might seem to be that the principles of substances are particular or individual and not universal. I develop this line of interpretation in the present chapter.

The correct understanding of Aristotle's *aporia* (and his response to it) is extremely important for our understanding of his theory of essences. For, on the interpretation I am proposing, the traditional view of Aristotelian essentialism, according to which essences are universal and associated with species, should be changed. According to the view I am proposing, Aristotle thought that the principles or essences of composite substances are individual or particular rather than universal.[15]

---

[15]This conclusion is controversial. It might be objected that the terminology in which the *aporia* is stated differs from the terminology in which the solution is stated. In the statement of the *aporia*, the contrast is between particular (καθ' ἕκαστον) and universal (καθόλου) principles, whereas the solution contrasts individual (τόδε τι) with universal principles. Some scholars have argued that Aristotle's solution to the *aporia* is that the principles are neither particular nor

Not surprisingly, the question concerning how to interpret Aristotle's treatment of the *aporia* has generated considerable scholarly dispute.[16] I shall discuss what I consider to be the most important difficulties for my interpretation, and hence the most important criticisms from scholars holding opposing views, later in the present chapter. But first, it is necessary to

---

universal, but τόδε τι, where to be τόδε τι is neither to be particular nor universal. See Joseph Owens, *The Doctrine of Being in the Aristotelian Metaphysics* (Toronto: Pontifical Institute, 1962); and Jonathan Lear's unpublished paper "Active Episteme," prepared for the Tenth Symposium Aristotelicum, Bern, 1984.

I translate "τόδε τι" as "individual" and reserve "particular" for "καθ' ἔκαστον." This translation, I believe, captures some of the associations of Aristotle's language. First, the phrase literally translates as "this something" or "a this" (see J. A. Smith, "τόδε τι in Aristotle," *Classical Review*, 35 [1921], 19). The demonstrative in both translations seems intended to pick out an individual, though not necessarily a material particular.

In the *Categories*, the phrase clearly picks out a material particular. There, the primary substances are individual men, horses, etc.: "Every substance seems to indicate an individual (τόδε τι). . . . [W]hat is shown is indivisible and one in number" (3b10ff.). Contrasted with primary substances are secondary substances (i.e., species), which Aristotle says, may seem to indicate an individual but really do not: "for the subject is not, as the primary substance is, one, but man and animal are said of many things" (3b17–19). The contrast drawn in this quotation mirrors the contrast drawn elsewhere between particulars and universals (*De. Int.* 17a38ff.; *Metaphysics* 999b34–1000a).

Even in Aristotle's mature metaphysics there is a close relationship between substance, being particular, and being individual. In *Metaphysics* VII.1, for example, the phrase "τόδε τι" is used to denote the category of substance; and, a few lines later, substance is called "particular," (1028a12, 27). The contrast between being universal and being individual is also retained in his mature thought (III.6 1003a5–12, VII.13). So, even though I agree that being individual is not simply equivalent to being particular in Aristotle's thought, and certainly not equivalent to being a material particular, I am not persuaded that if something is individual, then it is neither particular nor universal. Hence, I do not think this line of argument establishes that the correct interpretation of the resolution of Aristotle's *aporia* is that the principles of substances are neither universal nor particular.

[16]Alternative interpretations of *Metaphysics* XIII.10, and alternative resolutions of Aristotle's *aporia* are offered by Joseph Owens and Jonathan Lear (note 15) as well as by Robert Heinaman, "Knowledge of Substance in Aristotle," *Journal of Hellenic Studies*, 101 (1981), 63–67, and Walter Leszl, "Knowledge of the Universal and Knowledge of the Particular in Aristotle," *Review of Metaphysics*, 26 (Dec. 1972), 278–313. I discuss these papers in some detail in "Actual and Potential Knowledge in Aristotle" (forthcoming).

examine Aristotle's distinction between actual and potential knowledge in greater detail.

The distinction comes after a discussion of both wings of Aristotle's dilemma:

> The fact that all knowledge is universal, so that the principles of beings must be universal and not separate substances, contains the greatest problem among those mentioned, but nonetheless the statement is true in one way but not in another. For knowledge like knowing is of two kinds, of which one is in potentiality, the other in actuality. The potentiality (like matter) being universal and indefinite is of the universal and indefinite, but the actuality is definite and of a definite [thing], being an individual it is of an individual. Sight sees the universal color accidentally because this color which it sees is a color; and that which the grammarian contemplates, this *A*, is an *A*.
> [1087a10–21]

In this passage, Aristotle associates knowledge of the universal with potentiality and matter; he characterizes universal knowledge and its objects (i.e., universals) as "indeterminate." Actual knowledge, on the other hand, is "determinate" and individual, and so are its objects. I consider each of them in turn.

What, then, is the relationship among potentiality, matter, indeterminateness, and the universal? What ought to strike us as very odd in this cluster of ideas is the inclusion of the universal. For we are already familiar with the association in Aristotle's thought of the other three; in Chapter 4, I discussed potentiality and matter, and in § 1 of the present chapter I described Aristotle's tendency to say that matter is indeterminate and thus cannot be known. How does the universal fit here? A possible rationale for its inclusion can be found in a text from *Metaphysics* IX.7, in which Aristotle is discussing potentiality. He says that the proximate matter is always potentially the thing it becomes; e.g., wood is potentially a casket. And, Aristotle notes, we say that the casket is "wooden" and not "wood" because what the matter is when it is the matter-of-a-casket is that casket (potentially) and not some other thing (i.e., wood). From our discussion of the relationship between matter and form in the preceding chapter, we know that Aristotle thinks of the proximate matter as the potential casket, and that the proximate matter's definition is determined by the form of the casket. Aristotle invents a word, "thaten," which refers to any proximate matter.[17]

Aristotle extends this analysis of proximate matter to properties of objects in general:

> The universal and the substratum differ by being an individual or not being one; the substratum of properties is, for example, a man, a body and a soul, while the property is musical or pale (the subject is not called "music" when music comes to be in it, not "music" but "musical," and the man is not "pallor" but "pale," and not "walk" or "motion" but "walking" or "moving"—like the "thaten"). Whenever this is so, then the proximate subject is a substance; but when this is not so, but the predicate is a form and an individual, the proximate subject is matter and material substance. And it is only right that "thaten" would be used with reference to both the matter and to the properties; for both are indeterminates. [1049a27–b2][18]

Consider the proximate matter of a casket, wood. According to Aristotle, wood is potentially the casket (i.e., a determinate thing), but in itself it is indeterminate. Similarly, a universal property such as "pallor" is not a determinate thing. When we say "The casket is wooden" or "The man is pale," we are marking linguistically the distinction between the potentialities

---

[17]The word "thaten" translates Aristotle's "ἐκέινινον."

[18]I follow the best manuscripts (and Ps.-Alexander) and read "καθόλου" instead of O. Apelt's emendation "καθ'οὗ." For a discussion of the text, see W. D. Ross, *Aristotle's Metaphysics* (Oxford: Clarendon Press, 1924), vol. 2, p. 257. I believe that perfectly good sense can be made of the passage and that no change is required. When the subject is a substance, then it is an individual and, thus, is contrasted with a universal. When the subject is matter, then it, like the universal properties, is indeterminate. Even Ross, who accepts Apelt's emendation, understands the properties as being universals and, for that reason, indeterminate: "Pathe-[qualities] such as whiteness are indefinite not in the sense of having no character but in the sense of being "floating universals," not in themselves fixed down to any one substance but capable of belonging to any one out of many" (*Aristotle's Metaphysics*, vol. 2, p. 258). So, on either reading, the properties are universals and, for that reason, indeterminate.

of the proximate matter (wood) and the universal (pallor), and their respective actualities as the matter of a determinate thing and the qualification of a determinate thing. Viewed as proximate matter, wood is the potentiality for something being wooden; viewed as universal, pallor is the potentiality for something being pale.

In the passage we have been considering, proximate matter and universal properties are grouped together as potentialities, and are described as being "indeterminates." They become determinate through being the matter of, or the property of, a determinate individual, i.e., a substance. Considered in themselves they are indeterminate. Now what does "indeterminate" mean in this connection? In the case of the proximate matter, the indeterminateness can be understood in relation to form: what the matter (the potential casket) is, is determined by the form or actuality. Aristotle thinks that, owing to its matter, a composite substance contains a residue of indeterminateness, since matter is in itself indeterminate. But how does this explanation of indeterminateness, or any other explanation, apply to universals?

Aristotelian universals are indeterminate in two ways. First, Aristotle thinks that some universals *are* material composites, or at least are analogous to material composites. Second, universals are indeterminate because of their generality. Let us consider the first point. Aristotle seems to think that some universals are themselves composites of matter and form. For he says (*Metaphysics* VII.10) that universals such as man or horse, just like the individuals of which they are predicated, are composites of form and matter: "But man and horse and terms which are thus applied to individuals, but universally, are not substance but something composed of this particular formula and this particular matter treated as universal" (1035b27–30). Those universals which are predicated of composite entities are themselves composite; they have a material aspect. And if indeterminateness is a consequence of materiality, then these composite universals will be indeterminate, just as the individual material composite is, because of the matter. There is an obvious disanalogy between the way in

which a material individual is material and the way in which
a universal is material. For the individual is literally material
(an individual human being has a body), whereas the matter
"composes" the universal only in the sense of being a part of
its definition. But this disanalogy is not crucial, for it is precisely
concerning the issue of definition that the matter of the individual composite is problematic; matter is defined in relation
to form and is, in itself, indeterminate. Some Aristotelian universals, then, can be seen to suffer from the same definitional
indeterminacy as individual composite substances—and for the
same reason, even though these universals are not, of course,
literally material.

This explanation of the indeterminacy of universals applies
to only a certain range of universals: namely, those corresponding to composite individuals. This restriction does not exclude
the universals most important to my interpretation, however,
for it allows me to explain why Aristotle thinks that universal
essences corresponding to universal species-terms (e.g.,
"man" and "horse") are indeterminate and, hence, the objects
of potential knowledge. It explains why Aristotle thinks that
what the traditional interpretation considers to be essences are
really indeterminate entities.

As an interpretation of the passage we are considering, however, the limited range of universals is more problematic. For
Aristotle says not just that certain universals (because of their
material aspect) are indeterminate, but that universals generally are indeterminate. Now, it is possible that he was thinking
only of universals predicated of material composites, or that
he was perhaps thinking that every universal has a material
aspect in its definition. In the absence of strong evidence in
favor of either of these possibilities, however, it is necessary
to look for an additional explanation of the indeterminateness
of universals that would apply to every universal.

There is another source of indeterminateness in the universal—its generality. The universals are composed of "this particular formula and this particular matter treated as universal"
(1035b29–30). An individual man or horse, on the other hand,
is the compound of a particular soul and a particular body

(1037a5–10). The "parts" of the universal "man" are more general and indeterminate than the parts of the individual composite. When we consider the parts "as universal," we are moving to a level of generality and indeterminateness. The shift is from this soul and this body to this kind of soul and this kind of body. The universal can be "said of many things" precisely because of its generality; it can function as a principle of epistemic unity because of its generality and indeterminateness. Although I have illustrated the notion of indeterminateness as generality with examples of composite universals, it is perfectly clear that this notion of indeterminateness applies to any universal, whether it has a material component in its definition or not. So, the notion of generality provides an explanation for Aristotle's position that the universal—every universal—is indeterminate and, hence, the object of potential knowledge.

Actual knowledge, by contrast, is individual and determinate, and its objects are individual and determinate. In his examples of actual knowledge, Aristotle is concerned to make clear that the universal is *not* the object of knowledge. Again: "Sight sees the universal color accidentally because this color which it sees is a color; and that which the grammarian contemplates, this *A*, is an *A*." These illustrations of actual knowledge are problematic for a number of reasons,[19] but they are clearly intended to rule out the possibility that in actual knowl-

[19]The examples are problematic on at least two counts. First, Aristotle uses an instance of perception to illustrate a point about knowledge. The example must be taken as an analogy, not as an instance of knowledge. The analogy is suggestive, since the object of sight is always the individual color (e.g., a bit of blue) and not the universals (blueness or color). When we see an individual color, we are also seeing color, since the individual color is a color. The second example is also problematic, since it might suggest that the distinction between actual and potential knowledge in this passage should be interpreted in terms of a distinction drawn in *De Anima* 417a22–29. In that passage, Aristotle contrasts the possession of knowledge and the activity of knowing (i.e., the exercise of the knowledge possessed). Clearly, this distinction does not correspond to the one we are considering. For universals and individuals alike can be actively contemplated. The reason scholars have identified the two passages is that the example of the grammarian contemplating an individual *A* appears in both places. I criticize this interpretation, and several others, in my paper "Actual and Potential Knowledge in Aristotle" (note 16 above).

edge the objects known are universals. Universals enter the picture only because any individual has universals truly predicable of it.

According to this interpretation, the crucial difference between potential and actual knowledge is the difference between (i) knowledge that is less determinate and more general and (ii) knowledge that is more determinate and less general. And this difference is a consequence of the nature of the objects of potential and actual knowledge, i.e., of universals and individuals, respectively. Knowledge of an individual form or essence is more determinate than knowledge of a kind of form or essence. And because actuality stands to potentiality as form to matter, or as determinate to indeterminate, in Aristotle's thought, it makes sense for him to call knowledge of individuals "actual knowledge" and knowledge of universals "potential knowledge."

The account I have just given of the basis for Aristotle's distinction between potential and actual knowledge raises two central issues. The first issue is epistemological. On my view, Aristotle holds that we can have knowledge of individual principles. How does actual knowledge, the knowledge of individuals, fit into Aristotle's conceptions of knowledge and definition? The second issue concerns how we should understand the notion of an individual as it applies to the individual principles of substances. How ought we understand the concept of an Aristotelian individual form or essence? As I said earlier, serious difficulties with regard to either or both of these issues have led many scholars to disregard the distinction between potential and actual knowledge, or to interpret it differently. I discuss the epistemological problem in the remainder of this section, and the issue of how to understand the notion of an individual essence in § 4.

In Chapter 2, I described three central features of Aristotelian *epistēmē*: (i) knowledge is of principles andcauses; (ii) wisdom requires the grasp of first principles; and (iii) knowledge is systematic. According to my interpretation, actual knowledge is the grasp of individual principles of substances, and so actual knowledge appears to satisfy the first feature of Aristotelian *epistēmē*. If one knows what Socrates is by knowing what his soul or principle is, one's knowledge is explanatory; and, to that extent, it counts as *epistēmē*. Actual knowledge, as I have described it, is also compatible with features (ii) and (iii) of Aristotelian *epistēmē*, since it allows both for the existence of first or highest principles, the grasp of which would constitute wisdom, and for the idea that knowledge is systematic (i.e., that a grasp of first principles will provide for an understanding of the whole—of everything that is explained by them).

But is compatibility enough? It might be objected that, since the first principles of Aristotelian science are universal (e.g., the genus, the definition), clearly it is potential rather than actual knowledge that fully embodies these characteristics of Aristotelian *epistēmē*. Potential knowledge, the knowledge of universals, is the grasp of first principles (which, on this view, are universal), and so it provides systematic knowledge, i.e., knowledge of what is explained by the first principles. The fact that potential knowledge matches the characteristics of Aristotelian *epistēmē* is not problematic for my view; after all, potential knowledge, universal knowledge, is knowledge for Aristotle. What is problematic, however, is the claim that actual knowledge does not count as *epistēmē*, on the grounds that it could not be the grasp of first principles (which are universal) and, so, could not be systematic.

The question of whether or not actual knowledge could count as *epistēmē* turns on the question of whether or not all principles of Aristotelian science are universal. In the case of the science of being, or the science of substance, there is considerable reason to think they are not. For, as is well known, the first principle of Aristotle's cosmology is the first mover, the unmoved mover; "The first mover, then, of necessity exists; and insofar as it is necessary, it is good and, in this sense, a first principle" (*Metaphysics* 1072b10–11). "On such a principle, then, depend the heavens and the world of nature" (1072b14). The unmoved mover is an eternal substance and a pure actuality, which is the principle or source of the natural world.

Aristotle also appears to believe that there are additional unmoved movers that are responsible for the motions of the stars (1073a34–1073b1).

According to Aristotle, these eternal substances are prior to, and principles of, the substances we have been discussing—namely, essences and composite substances. It is beyond the scope of the present book to enter into a full discussion of this aspect of Aristotle's theory of substance. What is critical to notice for our purposes is that these substances are individuals and not universals. The science of substance, insofar as it is concerned with the first principles of substance, will be the study of individual first principles; ultimately, it will be the study of an individual first principle—the unmoved mover—rather than a genus or universal. So, in the context of the knowledge of substance, which is the context wherein Aristotle makes the distinction between potential and actual knowledge, we can explain quite concretely how actual knowledge, the knowledge of individuals, can be the knowledge of first principles and, therefore, how it can be systematic. In short, we can explain how actual knowledge can count as *epistēmē*.

There are, however, two features of Aristotelian epistemology that are less readily satisfied by individual principles. The first is the connection between the notion of a principle, or cause, and the notion of the universal in Aristotle's thought. As I explained in Chapter 2, Aristotle distinguishes between the knower and the experienced person on *two* grounds: the knower both grasps the cause or principle of a phenomenon *and* can make a universal judgment about phenomena of the same kind. Further, as I explained in § 1 above, Aristotle seems to think that the universal provides the principle of epistemic unity that grounds universal judgments. In relation to these features of Aristotelian *epistēmē*, individual principles appear to be inadequate for two reasons. First, they do not seem able to ground universal judgments. Knowledge of Socrates' individual essence, it might be claimed, gives us understanding of Socrates alone. Second, there is a difficulty concerning how we could formulate a definition of an individual essence, Socrates' essence, if all definition is intrinsically of universals.

The first apparent epistemic inadequacy of individual principles (or essences) is easier to address than the second. According to the first criticism of actual knowledge, it cannot count as *epistēmē* because, since it is of individuals, it does not provide a principle of epistemic unity upon which to base universal judgments. This point is correct, but unimportant, for it amounts to saying that actual knowledge cannot be *epistēmē* because it is not potential knowledge (knowledge of universals). The very notion of an epistemic principle of unity makes sense only if one is talking about knowing an indefinite number of individuals; so it is hardly surprising that it plays no role in actual knowledge, which is directed towards the individual— Socrates rather than all human beings.

The remaining epistemological issue concerns the topic of definition. How does the idea of individual principles fit with Aristotle's views on the nature of definition? Earlier, in Chapter 1, I said that Aristotelian definitions were characterized by two distinctive features: (i) definitions are of things, rather than words, and (ii) definitions are causal or explanatory. These two characteristics of Aristotelian definitions are equally satisfied by either universal or individual principles and, so, do not count for or against either interpretation.[20] But there is another characteristic of Aristotelian definitions. And it is difficult to understand how individual principles could satisfy feature (iii):

[20]Is the Aristotelian notion that definitions are causal or explanatory really neutral with regard to the question of whether the principles are individual or universal? After all, in Chapter 1, I said that it was by virtue of grasping the cause of some phenomenon (e.g., an illness) that a person could formulate a universal judgment. Further, that there is a close relationship between causes and universals is clear from other Aristotelian texts as well (e.g., *An. Post.* 88a5–6). If *all* causes simply are universals for Aristotle, then the essence must be universal as well, since it is the cause of being of substances. There is no indication, however, that *all* causes are universal for Aristotle. For he regularly cites an individual as the cause of a given phenomenon (e.g., the male parent as the efficient cause of the generation of an animal). How, then, should we understand the relationship between causes and universal judgments discussed in Chapter 1? Notice that the two items in question are a cause (with no specification of whether it is universal or individual) and a universal judgment. The grasp of a cause makes a universal judgment possible. On my view, the cause is not identical to the universal judgment, and it is entirely open whether the cause itself is universal or individual.

definitions are intrinsically common to or shared by a number of individuals; thus, they are of universals. Given this feature of Aristotelian definitions (which I discussed in § 1 above), it is hard to see how there could be definitions of individual principles. The issue is particularly critical in relation to the idea of individual essences. For, as we know, Aristotle characterizes definition as the account which states the essence.

So far as I know, there is no explicit discussion to be found elsewhere in Aristotle's texts that resolve the difficulty posed by Aristotle's remarks on the nature of definitions with respect to the idea of individual principles.[21] But it is quite easy to point out how Aristotle might have responded to the presumed incompatibility of his characterization of definitions as intrinsically shared by, or common to, more than one individual, on the one hand, and the idea of individual principles (i.e., individual objects of definition) on the other. Aristotle might have pointed out that from the fact that a given definition—say the definition of a human being—is common or shared, it does not follow that there are not individual humans whose definition it is. We know that Aristotle believes something like this, for we know that Aristotle believes that individual composite substances have definitions, and that they differ from nonsubstances in this regard. The fact that the definition of a human being is shared by a number of individuals, in this context, does not mean for Aristotle that the definition is not a definition of those individuals. We can apply the same position to the case of individual principles. From the fact that a definition of an individual principle could apply to a number of individual

[21]Alan Code emphasizes the issue of definition in his rejection of the "individual forms" interpretation in "The Aporematic Approach to Primary Being." The incompatibility between Aristotle's notion of definition and the "individual forms" interpretation led Code to devise an alternative interpretation according to which the principles (forms or essences) are shared, or common, but are not "universal" (as Aristotle defines the term). As common or shared, these forms can be objects of Aristotelian definitions; but since they are not universal, they are not prey to the arguments of *Metaphysics* VII.13. The difficulty with Code's proposal is that in this chapter (and elsewhere) Aristotle rejects not only the view that the principles of substances could be universal, but also that they could be shared or common (1038b9–12, 1040b20–27).

principles (because a definition is intrinsically capable of being shared), it does not follow that there is no definition of an individual principle. This way of responding to the problem of definition in connection with individual principles is Aristotelian, even though, as I stated above, it is not to be found explicitly stated in Aristotle.[22]

In describing how Aristotle might respond to the argument from definition, I used the example of an individual composite substance to show that it is plausible to attribute to him the view that there could be definitions of individual principles. But, even so, it is not yet clear how to understand Aristotle's view, for it is not yet clear what is meant by calling a principle or essence "individual."

4. Individual Essences in Aristotle

The question of whether or not it is plausible to attribute to Aristotle a theory of individual forms or essences turns in part upon the sorts of evidence discussed in the preceding three sections, but it also depends in part upon whether the notion of individual essences makes sense in an Aristotelian metaphysics. In this section, I address the latter issue.

According to the traditional interpretation of Aristotle, individual essences are not consistent with his views on indivi-

---

[22]In response to my Aristotelian account of how there could be definitions of individual essences, a defender of the species-essence interpretation might ask, "Do the individuals (substances or essences) have their definitions *directly* as individuals or *indirectly* as members of species or kinds?" My response is to rephrase the directly/indirectly contrast into Aristotelian language, in terms of causes. The cause of an individual substance having the definition it has is its form or essence. So, in a sense, the individual substance has its definition indirectly—not because of its species membership but because of its form or essence. The cause of a form or essence having the definition it has is itself. So, we could say that the essence has its definition directly because of what it is, and not because of its species membership. (The idea of species of forms or essences is quite strange and un-Aristotelian in any case.) Neither explanation requires an immediate reference to a species or species-essence. Rather, an individual substance's essence is the explanation for both (i) its definition and (ii) its species-membership.

duation.[23] The traditional picture is of a universal species-essence that is shared by individual members of the species. On this view, the principle of individuation of an individual composite substance is its matter and not its form or essence, which is universal. But if Aristotle's principle of individuation is matter, then it is hard to see how forms or essences *could* be individual. For, according to this view, the only possible individuals are material individuals; and since form and essence are not material individuals, they could not count as individuals for Aristotle.

Let us consider more carefully the claim that matter is Aristotle's principle of individuation. If this claim means that Aristotle thinks the cause of being of an actual individual substance is its matter, then it is wrong. Rather, as I argued in Chapter 4, Aristotle assigns that function to the essence. It is the form or essence that causes the matter to compose an individual—a determinate, unified substance. On the other hand, if the above claim means that those properties by which two individual substances of the same kind differ originate in their matter, then the claim is, roughly speaking, correct. This is what Aristotle means when he says that "when we have the whole, such a form in this flesh and bones, that is Callias or Socrates; and they are different because of their matter (for that is different), but the same in form (for the form is indivisible)" (VII.8.1043a5–8). In saying that Socrates and Callias are the same in form, but differ because of their matter, Aristotle could mean one of two things: (i) Socrates and Callias share one form and are individuated by matter (the traditional view); or (ii) their individual forms have the same features, and so the differences between them must be explained by their matter (my view). The forms or essences of two human beings do not explain the differences between them—that Callias is tall and beautiful, and Socrates is short and ugly, for example. Aristotle assigns that job to matter. But these material differences be-

[23]W. D. Ross explains this view very clearly in *Aristotle's Metaphysics*, vol. 1, p. cxv. Also see G. E. M. Anscombe, "The Principle of Individuation," in *Articles on Aristotle 3. Metaphysics*, ed. Jonathan Barnes, Malcolm Schofield, and Richard Sorabji (New York: St. Martin's Press, 1979), pp. 88–95.

tween two individuals are not what is responsible for their being two individual substances; that job is assigned to form, or essence.

As we have seen, the claim that matter is Aristotle's principle of individuation can be understood in either of two ways: (i) as a claim about how Aristotle explains the existence of individuals or (ii) as a claim about how Aristotle explains certain differences among individuals of the same kind. Since Aristotle does not use matter to explain the existence of individuals, there is no reason (at least no reason arising from his conception of an individual) to rule out nonmaterial individuals. The sense in which it is true to say that matter is Aristotle's principle of individuation does not pose a threat to the idea of individual forms or essences.

Even though individual forms or essences have not been ruled out by our discussion of individual composite substances, that discussion does suggest a couple of questions concerning individual forms or essences. First, in relation to the idea that form or essence is the principle that causes the matter to constitute an individual substance, we might ask "What causes the form or essence to be an individual?" Second, in relation to the idea that the differences in property of two composite substances are explained by their matter, we might ask, "What differentiates two forms or essences of the same kind?"

In several places where Aristotle describes forms or essences as individuals, he uses precisely the same term that he applies to material individual substances.[24] We do not find, however, in contrast to the case of composite individuals, any discussion of what causes them to be individuals. The reason for this is the same reason that Aristotle gives in connection with a very closely related issue: namely, the issue of the unity of immaterial substances. The issue of the unity of form or essence is closely related to the issue of their individuality because unity is one component of being an individual. Commenting on the unity of immaterial substances (e.g., essences), in contrast to

---

[24]Aristotle calls form or essence "individual" at *Metaphysics* v.8.1017b24–26; VIII.1042a29; IX.1049a35; XII.1070a11, 13–15; and at *De Gen. et Corr.* 318b32.

the unity of composite substances, Aristotle says: "But of the things which have no matter, either for reason or for sense, each is by its nature essentially a kind of unity. . . . [A]nd an essence is by its very nature a kind of unity as it is a kind of being. This is why none of these has any cause outside itself for being one, nor for being a kind of being" (VIII.6.1045a36–b5). Aristotle tells us here that there is no external cause, or no other cause, of an essence being one. It is just a basic unity. In the case of the composite substance, Aristotle appeals to form or essence to explain its unity; form and essence, he tells us here, are basic unities. Given Aristotle's position with respect to the issue of unity, it is very plausible to assume that he holds a similar position with respect to the closely related issue of individuality. For we know that Aristotle appeals to form or essence to explain the being of individual substances. It is very likely that he views forms or essences as basic individuals, and that he would deny that there is any external cause or principle of their being individuals.

Let us now consider the second question: What differentiates two essences of the same kind? As we know, Aristotle holds that matter is the origin of those properties which differ between two individual substances of the same kind. A natural question to ask is "How do two individual essences differ from one another?" One possible response is that they differ with respect to property. But this response seems to be precluded by certain of Aristotle's statements, such as the remark quoted above to the effect that the forms of Callias and Socrates are the same. Another possible response is that they differ by virtue of their being the forms or essences of different composite substances. The composite substance, on this view, functions just as matter does in relation to the composite. Neither the matter (in the case of the composite) nor the composite (in the case of form or essence) is a cause or principle of individuality. Rather, composite substances explain certain differences between the individual essences in question—e.g., that one is Socrates' essence and the other is Callias' essence. Although Aristotle does not address this issue directly, I believe that the second suggestion is faithful to his approach to the essences of individual substances.

Individual substances explain the differences between two essences of the same kind (e.g., two human essences) in a manner analogous to the way in which matter accounts for the differences between two individual substances of the same kind (e.g., two human beings). Does this explanation not cast doubt upon a central theme of my interpretation—that essences are the cause of being of individual substances? If I invoke individual substances to explain how one essence differs from another essence of the same kind (e.g., Socrates' essence from Callias' essence), then it would appear that individual substances are prior to essences in at least one respect. But, nothing very important (only accidental features) about the essence is explained by the individual substance, just as nothing very important about the individual substance is explained by matter. For example, Aristotle would use the individual substance to explain not the individuality of the essence (it just is a basic individual), but merely some of its accidental features (e.g., why it differs from another essence in spatio-temporal location). In contrast, the essence as the cause of being of the individual substance explains what the individual substance *is*, and not just its accidental features. Just as we would have no reason to call matter rather than essence the cause of being of an individual substance, we have no reason to call the individual substance the cause of being of its essence.

In the present chapter, I have completed my interpretation of Aristotle's essentialism. I have tried to show in some detail where my interpretation differs from the traditional view, and why it does so. My interpretation makes two basic claims, one concerning the *function* of essences and one concerning the *nature* of essences. I argued in Chapter 4 that the primary role of essences in Aristotle's theory of substance is causal, rather than classificatory. And I argued in the present chapter that the essences of composite substances are individual, rather than universal. In the next chapter, I shall compare this picture of Aristotelian essentialism with a contemporary theory of essences.

Chapter 6

ARISTOTLE AND KRIPKE

In the past decade, there has been a renewal of interest in "Aristotelian" essentialism, an interest initially sparked by Saul Kripke's already classic paper "Naming and Necessity."[1] In response, ancient philosophers have undertaken the task of comparing Aristotle's essentialism with the contemporary "Aristotelian" essentialism.[2] In the present chapter, I contribute to this comparative project by contrasting Aristotle's theory of essences with that of Kripke.

A contemporary philosopher, reading my account of Aristotle's essentialism, must be struck by its divergence from recent essentialist theories. Certain topics are missing. For example, I have said virtually nothing about possibility and necessity, the twin pillars of contemporary essentialist thought.

---

[1]First published in *Semantics of Natural Language*, ed. Donald Davidson and Gilbert Harman (Dordrecht: D. Reidel, 1972), pp. 253–355. A slightly revised version, with a new introduction, was published in book form: *Naming and Necessity* (Cambridge: Harvard University Press, 1980). The references that follow are to the book version.

[2]Three important papers are Nicholas White, "The Origins of Aristotle's Essentialism," *Review of Metaphysics*, 26 (Sept. 1972), 57–85; S. Marc Cohen, "Essentialism in Aristotle," *Review of Metaphysics*, 31 (March 1978), 387–405; and Joan Kung, "Aristotle on Essence and Explanation," *Philosophical Studies*, 31 (1977), 361–383.

Nor have I discussed the question of identity, which is fundamental to Kripke's essentialism. Other topics intrude. An example is the number of different roles Aristotle assigns to essence. Aristotle's essences are causes; they are the cause of being of individual material substances. Essences are actualities; they are the ends or goals that determine the being of composite substances. Essence, as the answer to the question "What is it?" corresponds to the definition of the object. Only the latter question appears to generate a list of necessary or essential properties that are recognizable to contemporary metaphysicians. (Even in this case, however, the similarity is only apparent since, as I discussed in Chapter 4, the Aristotelian definition does not comprise all of the object's necessary properties.)[3]

In the present chapter, I start from the fact that Aristotle's theory of substance and essence is strikingly different from Kripke's essentialism. I believe this approach is more fruitful and more accurate, both philosophically and historically, to one that would assimilate Aristotle to contemporary thought or vice versa. Before I can substantiate and develop my account of the differences between essentialism then and now, however, I must describe Kripke's views on essences.

1. A Sketch of Kripke's Essentialism

In his published writings, Kripke discusses at some length the essences of two different kinds of object: individuals (e.g., a human being or a tiger) and material stuffs (e.g., gold or

---

[3]I argued in Chapters 4 and 5 that Aristotle's essences are not properties of the objects whose essences they are. On my view, Socrates' form or essence is not a property of Socrates. This might appear to be a clear and important point of contrast between Aristotle and Kripke, since for Kripke an object's essence simply consists of its necessary properties. Indeed, I used to think this was an important point of difference (see my "Aristotelian Essentialism Revisited," *Journal of the History of Philosophy* [forthcoming]). I now think that this point of contrast rests upon an ambiguity, since it could be argued that Aristotle's position assumes a notion of property that Kripke's apparently does not.

water).[4] He also makes remarks which suggest that, on his theory, many other things turn out to have essences. For example, "being a pain" is a necessary or essential property of a pain.[5] Since my focus in the present book has been to explain Aristotle's theory of the essences of individual material substances, in this section I consider Kripke's reflections on the essences of material individuals. Examples of material individuals are members of natural kinds (e.g., tigers) and artifacts (e.g., lecterns).

Kripke frames the question of the essences of individual objects as follows: "Here is a lectern. A question which has often been raised in philosophy is: What are its essential properties? What properties, aside from trivial ones like self-identity are such that this object has to have them if it exists at all, are such that if an object did not have it, it would not be this object?"[6] Kripke's basic idea is to consider the properties of an object, (in this case, a lectern) and to reflect about those properties in relation to the identity of the object. Which properties are such that the lectern, if it lacked them, would not be this lectern? Those properties are the necessary or essential properties of the lectern. It is important to see that Kripke is not asking us to imagine what changes an object could undergo and still persist. Rather than thinking temporally about change, we are supposed to think modally. We should not ask, for example, "If the lectern becomes a hatrack, is it the same object?" Rather, we should ask, "If it is a lectern, could it be a hatrack and be the very same object?" The properties an object must have if it exists at all are the properties that, if the object did not have them, it would not be that very object. Kripke's essential properties of individual objects follow from our intuitions about their identity.

Kripke classifies the necessary properties of individual ob-

---

[4]In *Naming and Necessity*, Kripke discusses individuals at pp. 110–116, natural kinds and material substances at pp. 116–140.

[5]Ibid., p. 146.

[6]Kripke, "Identity and Necessity," in *Naming, Necessity, and Natural Kinds*, ed. Stephen Schwartz (Ithaca: Cornell University Press, 1977), p. 86.

jects into three sorts.[7] He does not claim that this list is exhaustive, nor does he claim that any individual object must have necessary properties of all three kinds. Even so, it is fruitful to think of the three sorts of essential properties as containing a theory, in rough outline, of the essences of material individuals:

(i) Properties of origin—A material object must be made from the very hunk of matter from which it was actually made; e.g., a table must be made from the very piece of wood from which it was made, and a person must originate from the very sperm and egg from which he or she actually did originate.

(ii) Sortal properties—"Being a table" is a necessary property of a table; the property "being a human being" is a necessary property of a human being.

(iii) Properties of substance—A material object must be made from the kind of matter from which, in fact, it is made; e.g., the wooden table is necessarily wooden. In what follows, to avoid terminological confusion, I refer to these properties as *material* properties, rather than properties of *substance*.

How does Kripke arrive at this list of necessary properties of individuals? He does so by referring to a particular by means of a rigid designator (i.e., an expression that refers to an object in all possible worlds in which it exists) and then reflecting on what properties that very object must have in order to be that very object.[8]

To see how the three kinds of necessary properties—origin, sortal, and material—could be determined for a given individual, let us consider the example of Queen Elizabeth. I begin

[7] See Kripke, *Naming and Necessity*, p. 114, n. 57.

[8] A possible world, for Kripke, is expressed by a contrary-to-fact conditional statement. On rigid designators, see Kripke, *Naming and Necessity*, pp. 3–15; on the correct way to think about possible worlds, see pp. 15–20. It is not necessary to investigate Kripke's semantic theories in any detail, since his essentialism is independent of those theories. For a very helpful and careful discussion of the latter point, see Nathan Salmon, *Reference and Essence* (Princeton: Princeton University Press, 1981).

by citing Kripke's explanation of why an individual's *origin* is necessary.

> How could a person originating from different parents, from a totally different sperm and egg, be *this very woman*? One can imagine , *given* the woman, that various things in her life could have changed: that she should have become a pauper; that her royal blood should have been unknown, and so on. One is given, let's say, a previous history of the world up to a certain time, and from that time it diverges considerably from the actual course. This seems to be possible. And so it's possible that even though she were born of these parents she never became queen. . . . But what is harder to imagine is her being born of different parents. It seems to me that anything coming from a different origin would not be this object.[9]

In determining which properties of a particular object are necessary, we are to imagine the history of the world in the vicinity of that object and then consider in which respects it could diverge from the actual history of the world and in which respects it could not.[10]

Consider Elizabeth II, queen of England. If she is to remain Elizabeth, some changes in her history are possible (and, hence, certain properties that Elizabeth actually has are not necessary or essential properties of her); some changes in her history are not possible (and, hence, certain of her properties are essential or necessary). The possibility or impossibility of changes in Elizabeth's history depends upon whether or not we would still say, envisioning a particular lost or gained property, that we are talking about *this very woman*. For example, it is possible to imagine that this very woman was never the queen of England (if, say, Edward VIII had not abdicated), but

---

[9]Kripke, *Naming and Necessity*, p. 113.

[10]Kripke is a bit more hesitant about this procedure for determining essences than my description might suggest: "Ordinarily when we ask intuitively whether something might have happened to a given object, we ask whether the universe could have gone on as it actually did up to a certain time, but diverge in its history from that point forward so that the vicissitudes of that object would have been different from that time forth. *Perhaps* this feature should be erected into a general principle about essence" (ibid., p. 115, n. 57).

it is not possible to imagine that this very woman was born of different parents from her actual parents.

This claim turns upon our intuitions about the identity of individual persons. The genetic contribution of the parents appears basic to the identity of the offspring, in contrast to the various attributes that attach to the person during his or her life. What does this intuition amount to? We can imagine a slight alteration in the history of the universe so that the genetic material differs from the actual genetic material. Say the queen has green eyes instead of blue eyes. It seems to me that this property would be treated like the property "being the queen of England"—namely, as a contingent property of Elizabeth. And it seems to me that a considerable portion of the properties associated with the genetic material from Elizabeth's parents could also change, and the result would be *this very woman*. If one's intuition about the identities of individual persons permits wide variation in the properties associated with their life histories, the very same intuition should permit a rather liberal tampering with their genes.

It follows from the foregoing that it does not matter what the "content" of the genetic material is—so long as it is the very genetic material from which the person did in fact spring. What is important is the causal chain, Elizabeth's genealogy. The necessity of origin means that if a person originates from a particular egg and sperm, then he or she must have originated from that very egg and sperm. I have said that the genetic material in the egg and sperm could be quite different. One might ask, "What counts as the same egg and sperm?" Well, they must be the very pair from which Elizabeth did come, whichever pair that might turn out to be.

There is some limit, however, on the sperm and egg. That limit is imposed in part by the necessity of *sortal properties*. Elizabeth must have originated in a human sperm and egg. Many properties of Elizabeth could change, and we would still have *this very woman*, but "being a human being" is not one of them. Imagine an alteration in the history of the world in Elizabeth's vicinity such that Elizabeth is not a human being, but a Vulcan. Kripke would hold that, in this case, our identity intuition tells us that the Vulcan would not be Elizabeth (given, of course, the assumption that Elizabeth is a woman, a human being).

Kripke also thinks that *material properties* are essential or necessary properties. Consider a wooden table. The necessity of origin tells us that the table was necessarily made of the very piece of wood from which it was actually made. The necessity of matter says that the table must have been made of wood. In the case of Queen Elizabeth, the necessity of origin tells us that she must have originated from the very egg and sperm from which she did originate. The necessity of matter says that she must be made out of protoplasm rather than, say, plastic.

One additional aspect of Kripke's essentialism deserves comment because it will provide an important point of contrast with Aristotle. Kripke holds that the essences of material individuals can be determined independently from the question of the metaphysical constitution of individuals such as persons, artifacts, or organisms. What he does say about individuals is negative: "What I do deny is that a particular is nothing but a "bundle of qualities," whatever that may mean. If a quality is an abstract object, a bundle of qualities is an object of an even higher degree of abstraction, not a particular."[11] Kripke also denies an alternative view which holds that there is a "bare particular" or "propertyless substratum" underlying the properties.

Individuals such as tables and persons are not bundles of propeties, nor are they bare particulars clothed in properties. Kripke's reason for denying the "bundle" view is that the object in that case would not be a particular. He does not state any specific reason for rejecting the "bare particular" view. Rather, he thinks that both views are the consequence of a mistaken line of reasoning:

> Philosophers have come to the opposite view through a false dilemma: they have asked, are these objects *behind* the bundle of qualities, or is the object *nothing but* the bundle? Neither is the case; this table is wooden, brown, in the room, etc. It has

[11]Ibid., p. 52.

all these properties and is not a thing without properties, behind them; but it should not therefore be identified with the set, or 'bundle', of its properties. Don't ask: how can I identify this table in another possible world except by its properties? I have the table in my hands, I can point to it, and when I ask whether *it* might have been in another room, I am talking by definition about *it*.[12]

Kripke's remarks about the ontological constitution of individual objects come in the context of a discussion of the problem of transworld identification: How do I identify this table in some other possible world? Do I do so using the table's properties—or a subset of its properties, e.g., its essential properties? The idea of identifying the table in other possible situations in purely qualitative terms is inadequate, Kripke says, because the particular, *this table*, is not a bundle of qualities or properties. Kripke also thinks, however, that this way of framing a problem about the transworld identity of particulars is misguided and unnecessary, because "we begin with the objects, which we *have*, and can identify, in the actual world. We can then ask whether certain things might have been true of the objects."[13]

What is most interesting in this discussion is that Kripke rejects two metaphysical analyses of what individual objects are but does not offer any alternative account. It is clear that he does not think any general theory of the nature of individuals is required in order to ask about their essential or necessary properties.

Does Kripke think that material individuals such as tables and persons are entirely unreceptive to further analysis? No, he does not. For Kripke allows that we can analyze these individuals into other individuals, e.g., the molecules that compose them:

Similarly, given certain counterfactual vicissitudes in the history of the molecules of a table, *T*, one may ask whether *T* would exist, in that situation, or whether a certain bunch of molecules,

[12]Ibid., pp. 52–53.
[13]Ibid., p. 53.

which in that situation would constitute a table, constitute the very same table *T*. In each case, we seek criteria of identity across possible worlds for certain particulars in terms of those for other, more "basic," particulars.[14]

The scarequotes appear around the word "basic" because Kripke is uncommitted on this point, i.e., about whether or not molecules are in a metaphysical sense "more basic" than tables. Tables can be identified in terms of their constituents (molecules) and, in this sense, are not basic; but this fact does not carry any metaphysical weight. Molecules, the constituents of tables, are not ontologically privileged (or, in our terminology, ontologically basic beings). For:

Unless we assume that some particulars are "ultimate," "basic" particulars, no type of description need be regarded as privileged.[15]

Kripke rejects two views of the ontological constitution of individual objects: the "bundle of properties" view and the "bare particular" view. Tables and persons are not incomposites, however, for they are composed from bunches of molecules, bunches of particulars. Molecules, nonetheless, are not more basic or ultimate than tables or persons in any important metaphysical sense. Neither, however, are tables or persons ontologically privileged. Most important for our comparison with Aristotle is Kripke's idea that we can determine the essences of given individuals independently of saying either what an individual is or what the ontologically basic individuals are.

2. Essence, Identity, and Definitions

Aristotelians will have noticed something familiar about Kripke's intuitive reflection on the identity of individual objects—persons, artifacts, organisms. These reflections yield

[14]Ibid., p. 50.
[15]Ibid., p. 51.

necessary or essential properties of (i) origin, (ii) kind, and (iii) matter. These three sorts of essential properties roughly correspond to three of Aristotle's four causes: (i) efficient, (ii) formal, and (iii) material.[16]

It is very interesting that there is some correspondence between the sorts of essential properties cataloged by Kripke and the explanatory factors propounded by Aristotle. Given this apparent coincidence of intuitions concerning material substances, it is even more interesting to ask why Aristotle excludes material and efficient causes from the essence of material substances. Why not include these elements in the definition of material substances and, thereby, include them in its essence? The answer to this question is different in the two cases. Properties of origin are not essential for Aristotle, because he determines what is essential not by reflecting on the identity of an individual, but by considering how to define the individual. The exclusion of matter or material properties from the Aristotelian definition and essence has another origin: namely, the roles of essence as cause of being and of actuality. Each of these differences, then, is a consequence of a more basic difference in the two essentialisms. Let us consider each of them further.

By including the "origin of the motion," or the efficient cause, among four causal factors by means of which we are to understand material substances, Aristotle acknowledges the importance of its source or origin in the causal history of the substance. What an object actually "comes from" seems to be central to our understanding of it—hence, the importance of genealogies for human beings, pedigrees for animals, and so on. On a more abstract level, material substances are such that there must be some origin for their generation; they do not pop into existence from nothing, they do not generate them-

---

[16]The fact that there is no Kripkean analogue to Aristotle's final cause reveals a basic difference with respect to how each philosopher thinks of essences. It is an inherent part of Aristotle's view that essences are teleological, for he identifies formal and final causes. There is no trace of teleology in Kripke's essentialism.

selves, they are not eternal. So, Aristotle thinks we should always look for the origin or source of the generation.

Why does the origin or source of the material substance turn out to be an essential property of the material substance for Kripke, but not for Aristotle? Why is it just an explanatory or causal factor, in our understanding of material substances for Aristotle, and an essential property for Kripke? I have just pointed out that, roughly speaking, the two philosophers share an intuition about the importance of origin in the causal history of substances, so the explanation cannot be simply that Aristotle does not think this factor is important. But if this is so, why would Aristotle reject (as he certainly would) Kripke's position that a material individual's origin is essential to it?[17]

The answer to this question points toward a basic difference in the two essentialisms: namely, that Aristotle does not derive his essences from reflecting upon the identity of individual substances. His essentialism does not emerge from a determination, with respect to a given individual substance such as Socrates, of which properties could change and still leave us with the very same person. The essential properties of origin, which result from this procedure, are radically individual essential properties. A radically individual essential property is just an essential property that is peculiar to a given individual; each human being has a different essential property of origin.[18]

Aristotle's essentialism is not based on the idea of individual identity but is tied to his notion of definition. Essences provide the answer to the question "What is it?" And there is no ob-

---

[17]Are Kripke and Aristotle really at odds with regard to the question of the necessity of origin? Since Aristotle distinguishes between the essence and necessary properties, an object's origin could be one of its necessary properties without being included in its essence. On this view, the difference between Aristotle and Kripke does not concern the necessity of properties of origin, but rather Aristotle's position that not all necessary properties are essential. Although it is *possible* that Aristotle thought that properties of origin are necessary (but not essential), and hence it is possible that he does not differ from Kripke on this point, there is no evidence that Aristotle did think that properties of origin are necessary. So, the most plausible interpretation is that for Aristotle properties of origin are neither essential nor necessary.

[18]The phenomenon of identical twins poses a difficulty for Kripke's views, since each twin originates from the same egg and sperm.

vious link between that question, which asks for a definition of the object, and the object's source or origin. So, it is perfectly conceivable that one could define an object without reference to its origin. But, if this is so, then Aristotle would have no reason to include the origin in an object's essence. Further, the radical individuality of essential properties of origin makes them unsuitable for inclusion in an Aristotelian essence. What is the difference between the "radically" individual essences I attribute to Kripke and the individual forms or essences that (I argued in earlier chapters) figure in the correct understanding of Aristotle's essentialism? On Aristotle's view, the individual forms or essences of two human beings could be specified in a single definition, the definition of a human being (see Chapter 5, § 3). On Kripke's view, however, the essences of two human beings would differ with respect to their property of origin; there could be no single definition that would specify both essences (where those essences are composed of all of their necessary properties). In short, since the identity of individuals is not the central concept of Aristotle's essentialism, as it is of Kripke's, properties that are essential by virtue of their role in constituting a given individual object's identity need not count as essential for Aristotle.

Aristotle and Kripke also differ with regard to the essentiality of matter. For Kripke, but not for Aristotle, objects such as artifacts have essential, or necessary, material properties. Consider Kripke's lectern. It is made out of wood; it is a wooden lectern. Nothing could be that wooden lectern without being wooden and being a lectern. Hence, we get Kripke's essential properties of matter and kind. Aristotle also frequently uses an artifact to illustrate a similar distinction in his thought between matter and form. The brazen sphere is compounded out of matter and form. Material substances quite generally are compounds of matter and form. Indeed, as we saw in Chapter 3, Aristotle insists that the student of nature will try to grasp both material and formal causes when trying to understand a material substance. Yet Aristotle does not include matter in the definition of a composite substance; the definition, he holds, is a determination of the form and actuality. Since the definition of the substance corresponds to its essence, matter and material properties are excluded from the essence. Why is the definition of a material substance a definition of its form and not its matter? Why could the definition not be a definition of both?

Before answering this question, it is important to see that Aristotle's exclusion of matter and material properties from the essence provides additional evidence for the view that Aristotle does not base his essentialism on the identity of individual substances. For, if he did, then matter would turn out to be essential. Surely, it would be clear to Aristotle that in order to be *this very brazen sphere*, an object would have to be brass. To hold that Aristotle is deriving essences from identity *and* excluding material properties would be plausible only if one attributed to him some very strange intuitions about the identity of individual objects. For example, one would have to attribute to Aristotle the view that an object could be *this very brazen sphere* and be made out of glass. It is much more plausible to hold that he does not derive essences in this way.

But, even if Aristotle does determine what is to count as essential by considering the object's definition and not its identity, it is still puzzling why he thinks that the definition, and hence the essence, should not include reference to the object's matter as well as to its form. After all, a brazen sphere or a human being is a composite of matter and form. Why not define them with a "composite" definition, one that makes reference to matter as well as to form or essence. Why does Aristotle hold that the definition is the definition of the form?

Matter and form (or essence) are not two equal, independent factors in the constitution of an Aristotelian composite substance. They are not equal partners because its form or essence, not its matter, is the cause of being of the substance. They are not independent partners because matter is potential being that is determined by an essence or actuality. Since form or essence is the cause of being of a substance, it makes sense to hold that form or essence, rather than matter, is much more important for the definition of the substance. But, it might be argued, although form or essence is much more important for the definition of the substance, it does not follow that its matter has no contribution to make. So, the fact that its form or essence and not its matter is the cause of being of the substance does not entirely rule out the claim of matter for inclusion in the definition. In order to rule out matter's claim entirely, we must add Aristotle's analysis of matter and form (or essence) as potentiality and actuality. Here the point is not just that form or essence is much more important in the constitution of the substance than matter. Rather, the characterization of matter as potentiality and of form as actuality, as we saw in an earlier chapter, means that the form or essence determines what the matter is (Chapter 4, § 5). So, matter does not have any independent contribution to make to the definition and essence of the substance. In light of Aristotle's description of essence as the cause of being and the actuality of material substances, his exclusion of matter or material properties from their essences can be understood.

Aristotle's reasons for excluding matter or material properties from the essences of material substances are a consequence of his analysis of what an individual material substance is. In other words, his doctrines that essence is (i) the cause of being and (ii) the actuality of material substances have a direct impact on the essences of given individuals. It is because essences play these roles in his analysis of individual material substances—and because, as a consequence of this analysis, matter is excluded from essences—that material properties, according to Aristotle, are not essential properties of material substances such as Queen Elizabeth and the lectern. If a material substance is an hylomorphic compound, and if form or essence is its cause of being and actuality, then when one says what it is, one will be giving an account of its form or essence, not its matter.

3. Essence and Individuals

The second fundamental point of difference between Aristotle and Kripke concerns how, on each view, the theory of essence is connected to the question of the ontologically basic beings. This, for Aristotle, is really the question of the ontologically basic individuals, or substances. As I explained in the first section of the present chapter, however, Kripke does not connect these two questions. He does not think that one needs to connect one's theory of essences to a theory of the individual, or a theory of basic individuals. In order to understand the importance of this difference, then, it is necessary to see why Aristotle does connect the two issues.

One way to begin to grasp Aristotle's approach is to recall a distinction I made on Aristotle's behalf (Chapter 1) between the definitional question and the population question. The question "What is substance?" can be approached in two ways—as asking the population question (which things are substances?) or as asking the definitional question (What is it to be a substance?). Aristotle says that a resolution of the definitional question will help clarify and resolve the population question. The population issue is ambiguous, however; for at the very outset Aristotle provides a lengthy list of candidates, some everyday and some the fruit of theory, for being substance. Right at the outset we can point to substances. Nonetheless, our developed answer to the definitional question will have consequences for the list with which we began. We will no longer consider the parts of animals and plants to be substances, for example.

Why and how is the question of essence connected to the questions concerning population and definition? The definitional question concerns the nature of substance, and, as I have just explained, Aristotle thinks that a resolution of the population question will ultimately require an analysis of the nature of substance. Indeed, in *Metaphysics* vii–ix, Aristotle analyzes the nature of substance by considering the nature of material substances. According to his account, matter constitutes an actual, individual substance because of the presence of essence. Conversely, he argues that only substances, entities with a high degree of unity and determination, have essences in the full sense.

The important point is that, for Aristotle, the population question is genuinely problematic. Which of the entities he lists really are substances is not obvious, even though some of his candidates are ordinary objects such as animals and plants.

Even if we grant that the population question is difficult, it is still not clear why that issue is connected with a determination of essence. Why does the determination of essence presuppose an answer to the population question? Why do we have to figure out which are the ontologically basic beings prior to, or at least concurrently with, our account of essences? Why can we not separate the question of substance (comprising both the population and the definitional question) from the issue of essence? Why can we not consider individuals (e.g., lecterns and animals) and determine their essences, without addressing any larger ontological issues?

Consider an artifact, the lectern. Why, according to Aristotle, is it not correct simply to ask about its essential properties? Aristotle's idea is that one needs to know whether the artifact is something, or not, over and above its matter. If the lectern is nothing but its matter, for example, then its essence will be the essence of the matter that composes it. Or, consider a natural substance, say, an animal. Is a part of the animal (e.g., the heart) ontologically basic or not? The answer to this question will have consequences for how one thinks about the definition of the whole animal and how one thinks about the definitions of its parts. And since the definition states the essence, it will also have consequences for essences. The connection between substance and essence is just that a specification of what it is whose definition and essence is in question is necessary.

The phrase "specification of what it is" is ambiguous. I do not mean a merely linguistic specification. That is not enough; for a linguistic specification ("the lectern I am pointing to") leaves open the question of whether or not the lectern is ontologically basic. Further, it is not enough to follow our intuitions in a given case. The suggestion is that our intuitions about essential properties in given cases (e.g., the lectern) will tell us whether or not it is ontologically basic. But, this is not right. Our intuitions about essential properties will reflect a view of what the lectern is, of course, but the properties will only be essential *given that view*. In order to remove the relative or hypothetical character from the essential properties, it is necessary to determine whether or not the lectern is ontologically basic. But this decision must be prior to, or at least concurrent with, questions about the essence, since it has consequences for what could be an essential property of the object.

The explanation of Aristotle's approach to the question of essence—namely, that essences are specified within a theory of substance, which is to say within a theory of being—makes use of his particular analysis of material substance. However, the basic point does not rely upon Aristotle's specific answer to the question "What is being?" Rather, the point is that some answer to that question, some account of what is ontologically basic, is or should be an integral part of any essentialist theory.

This point can serve as a conclusion to both this chapter and this book. As a conclusion to my contrast of Aristotle with Kripke, the idea that a theory of essences should be developed within a theory of what is ontologically basic is fitting: there is a fundamental difference, not simply of results but of approach, between the two essentialisms. Since this difference is basic and central, I believe that it can both help explain the apparent strangeness of Aristotle's discussions of essence to contemporary philosophers as well as explain the vague feeling on the part of Aristotle specialists such as myself that a contemporary essentialist such as Kripke is engaged in a very different project from Aristotle's.

This description of Aristotle's approach to essences also serves as a fitting conclusion to my book, since it links together themes from earlier chapters. It might well have occurred to the reader to ask why, in a book on Aristotelian essences, we began with a general account of Aristotle's approach to the question of being. The idea that the population question is problematic for Aristotle (together with the relationship of that question to the question of being) was discussed in Chapter 1. Aristotle's idea that we can study being by studying the ontologically basic beings, or substances, was explored in Chapter 2. We can now see the direct, theoretical connection between these topics, on the one hand, and what Aristotle has to say about essences and material substances, on the other. Moreover, we can now see the magnificence and breadth of Aristotle's undertaking in the *Metaphysics*—namely, to construct a theory of being—and we can appreciate his doctrine of essences as one part of that theory.

INDEX

Library of Congress Cataloging-in-Publication Data

Witt, Charlotte, 1951-
  Substance and essence in Aristotle : an interpretation of
Metaphysics VII-IX /Charlotte Witt.
    p. cm.
  Includes index.
  ISBN 0–8014–2126–8 (alk. paper)
  1. Aristotle. Metaphysics. 2. Metaphysics. 3. Essence
(Philosophy) 4. Aristotle—Contributions in essentialism.
I. Title.
B434.W58 1989
111'.1—dc19   88–24043

Printed in the United States
203682BV00001B/322-372/P